PERFECT PHRASES™

for

SALES
REFERRALS

Other titles in the *Perfect Phrases* series include:

Perfect Phrases for Performance Goals, Second Edition
by Douglas Max and Robert Bacal

Perfect Phrases for Customer Service, Second Edition
by Robert Bacal

Perfect Phrases for Managing Your Small Business
by Robert Bacal and Nancy Moore

Perfect Phrases for the Sales Call, Second Edition
by Jeb Brooks and William Brooks

Perfect Phrases for Referrals and Getting New Clients
by Jeb Brooks and Marty Scirratt

Perfect Phrases for Lead Generation by William Brooks

Perfect Phrases for Business Proposals and Business Plans
by Don Debelak

Perfect Phrases for Meetings by Don Debelak

Perfect Phrases for Real Estate Agents and Brokers
by Dan Hamilton

Perfect Solutions for Difficult Employee Situations by Sid Kemp

Perfect Phrases for Executive Presentations by Alan Perlman

Perfect Phrases for Coaching Employee Performance
by Laura Poole

PERFECT PHRASES™

for

SALES

REFERRALS

**Hundreds of Ready-to-Use Phrases
for Getting New Clients, Building Relationships,
Increasing Your Sales**

Jeb Brooks and Marty Scirratt

New York Chicago San Francisco Lisbon London Madrid Mexico City
Milan New Delhi San Juan Seoul Singapore Sydney Toronto

1 2 3 4 5 6 7 8 9 10 QFR/QFR 1 9 8 7 6 5 4 3

ISBN   978-0-07-181008-1
MHID   0-07-181008-0
e-ISBN 978-0-07-181009-8
e-MHID   0-07-181009-9

This is a CWL Publishing Enterprises Book developed for McGraw-Hill by CWL Publishing Enterprises, Inc., www.cwlpub.com.

Library of Congress Cataloging-in-Publication Data

Brooks, Jeb.
  Perfect phrases for sales referrals : hundreds of ready-to-use phrases for getting new clients, building relationships, and increasing your sales / by Jeb Brooks, Marty Scirratt.
    pages cm
  Includes bibliographical references and index.
  ISBN-13: 978-0-07-181009-8 (alk. paper)
  ISBN-10: 0-07-181009-9 (alk. paper)
1. Selling. 2. Business referrals. 3. Business communication. I. Scirratt, Marty. II. Title.
  HF5438.25.B7425 2013
  658.8'10014--dc23

                                      2013004869

McGraw-Hill Education books are available at special quantity discounts to use as premiums and sales promotions or for use in corporate training programs. To contact a representative, please e-mail us at bulksales@mcgraw-hill.com.

Contents

Introduction

Rick sells industrial equipment to manufacturers. Right now, he only has one potentially worthwhile opportunity to pursue, but it's a long shot. He has been calling his contact inside the account every day for a week to "check in" and get an update. Even though there really are not any buying signals, Rick still sees them everywhere. He is looking for the silver lining in what is quickly turning into a storm cloud. Finally, fed up, his contact tells him they are going with a competitor, insists that Rick stop calling, and hangs up on him. Rick has nothing else to rely on. He has no choice but to start cold calling.

Sarah sells for the same company in a neighboring territory. Just as Rick is getting hung up on, she is wrapping up a meeting with a prospect to whom a current client eagerly introduced her. Later this afternoon, she will head to a meeting with a major manufacturer who is interested in committing to a purchase that would mark Sarah's biggest sale ever. She was introduced by a mutual friend—an architect—whom Sarah met at a trade show. Because Sarah knows precisely what to say and how to ask for referrals, she is never at a loss for opportunities. She practically has a river of referrals flowing to her.

Imagine what that's like! Rivers of referrals flowing into your office every day! It is possible. And it's a lot easier—and more effective—than making thousands of cold calls. Unfortunately, many salespeople seem unwilling to do the work required to identify, cultivate, and benefit from those referral sources we call connectors. A *connector* is someone who can introduce you to new opportunities.

Which salesperson are you most like? Are you Rick? Struggling for prospects and opportunities? Or are you Sarah? Managing the many referrals and new prospects that come to you?

Sarah has a full funnel. And it is full because she learned exactly what to do and precisely what to say to generate referrals. She is a truly professional salesperson who leads a successful career. And this kind of professional life is possible (even likely) if you learn the strategies and tactics in this book. Simply put, you do not have to cold call for the rest of your life. We tell you more about Sarah in Chapter 1.

What This Book Can Do for You

By using this book you can generate more referrals, leading to more qualified prospects and leading to more customers. By putting the phrases we present into your daily sales-speak, you will find that you have more qualified prospects who will gladly meet with you. Further, you will interact with them in a way that will not be annoying or distracting. You will take strides toward becoming a trusted advisor.

It doesn't matter if you are new to sales, to your company, to the neighborhood, to the product, or to the territory. Learn these strategies and phrases and get ready for your professional life to become what you've always wanted!

This book is divided into three parts. The first part provides the background about referrals. It explains why most salespeople have a tough time earning them. This first part also offers you specific strategies and language to use to combat the most common challenges. Part II explains the best, overarching strategy for earning a steady stream of referrals. It is called Give-to-Get, and if you really understand and truly adopt it, you will have an almost unstoppable flood of referrals coming to your desk. The third and final section of the book outlines specific phrases to use with specific types of connectors (i.e., the people who can provide you with referrals). We provide phrases for speaking on the phone, in face-to-face meetings, on e-mail, and even for social media. We show you exactly how to ask for referrals in the preferred language for 38 types of prospects. In Chapter 10, we give you a strategy—proven by some of the most successful referral generators to be incredibly powerful.

If you are looking for short-term strategies to earn referrals, pay particular attention to Chapters 6, 7, and 8. If you are in it for the long-term, read Chapter 10. However, the best strategy is to combine both our short-term strategies and our long-term approach. That will guarantee an abundance of referrals and will be the best strategy for maximum return on your investment of time, energy, and effort.

PART

PERFECT PHRASES FOR EARNED REFERRAL FACTOR

CHAPTER 1

How a Referral-Based Business Can Work

To show you what's possible, we'd like to take a few pages to share a story about how one salesperson built a river of referrals.

Calvin's new boss approached him and reached out to shake his hand. "Calvin, I'm glad you're on our team. You've done well for your first month with us," he said.

Calvin's boss seemed to be a good sales manager. He appeared to have control over what was happening in his office and with his sales team. The new hire training class he led Calvin through over his first month had been intense. But like a lot of salespeople being holed up behind a desk for weeks, Calvin was ready to get out of the office and into the real world. He hadn't been told his agenda for his second month.

"I hope you've enjoyed your first month. I'm impressed with how quickly you picked up on our products. Coming into a new industry can take some getting used to. You deserve a relaxing weekend. Over the next week I want you to tag along with Sarah Miller, our number-one sales rep for the last four years. If there's anyone here in our sales organization who understands how to create sales, it's Sarah."

"What makes her so good?" Calvin asked, anticipating a complicated answer.

The boss exhaled deeply. This wasn't the first time he had been asked this question. And he knew exactly how to answer it, because he did know what made Sarah stand out from the rest of the sales team. The problem was, none of the new sales reps took his advice seriously. It wasn't that he was reluctant to tell Calvin Sarah's secret; rather, he was remembering the last four rookie reps who tagged along with her. It was like they had selective hearing.

The boss looked at Calvin, looked down at the floor, and looked up again, making sure Calvin was looking into his eyes. "Here's Sarah's secret. She never runs out of people and prospects to talk with. You've heard of the best salespeople having not only a stream but a whole river of referrals? She does. Understand, she's not the best when it comes to product information. She's not even my best closer. But she knows how to get the referrals. And more important, at least for her and our business, she knows how to convert those referrals into sales."

"Thanks, boss! I appreciate that you are letting me learn from the best," Calvin said enthusiastically. "Tell me, what's the one thing I want to be looking for as I tag along with Sarah during this next week?"

"That's a great question, Calvin. Asking good questions is a great start at being successful in sales. And I know exactly what you should be observing. But rather than just giving it to you, perhaps a better way for you to truly learn is for you to watch and think about it for the first couple of days with her. Then let's talk and see what you've discovered."

"Okay, then," Calvin agreed, a little surprised. He really wanted to be able to zero in on her secret. Now he would have to work a little harder for the answer. Regardless, though, he sensed that his next week was going to be quite a ride.

"I'll make sure Sarah knows you will be at her office at 8:30 Monday morning," the boss said. "And you'll find Sarah is punctual. I wouldn't be late, if I were you."

Calvin made sure he arrived a little early to meet Sarah on Monday morning. He wanted to make a good impression on her. After all, she was the number-one salesperson for the company." Nothing like a little goodwill to start the week," he said to himself while walking into the sales office area. With new hire training in a different building, he had only been to his cubicle on the first day of his job.

He rounded the corner and saw his workspace for the second time. It seemed smaller than he remembered. Oh, well. As he turned his chair around to sit, he saw a note in the seat. "Meet me in Conference Room B at 8:30. I have a conference call to begin our week. —Sarah"

Looking around, he saw a wall of small conference rooms, all with four chairs around a large table. He walked past several conference rooms before arriving at B. Looking through the door's window, Calvin saw Sarah. Well, he saw her back. She was sitting in the chair nearest the door. Trying to be polite, Calvin knocked lightly. Sarah turned around, opened the door, and immediately reached out her hand and said, "You must be Calvin. I'm Sarah."

Introducing himself, Calvin accepted Sarah's invitation to sit as she began their discussion of his new role as her shadow salesperson.

She continued, "Welcome to the team. Our manager was quite impressed with you over the last four weeks and asked me to show you the ropes, so to speak. I'm glad you'll be with me. I have two rules for our time together. One, if I ask you to do something, you'll do it, and do it immediately. I don't want you to ask a ton of questions about why you should do something. Just do it. Then, after the task is done, you can ask all the questions you want.

"Second, you will work as hard as I do during our time together. You might believe that you're just along for the ride. That's not it at all. You are here to learn, and I've always believed the best way to learn is to do. So, if I'm working, I want you to be working. There won't be enough time for you to check on the status of your fantasy football team. Nor time for you to catch up on your friends' latest posts on Facebook. With that said, there is always time to communicate with your family or take care of emergencies. Any questions?"

Calvin stood there, a little stunned. Sarah was all business, a severe departure from the casual, laidback approach to sales training he'd experienced with past employers.

Realizing he hadn't replied, he assured her, "No, no questions. That sounds fair enough."

"Good," she answered. "Now, sit down here and let me show you what we're going to accomplish today."

Sarah appeared to be an excellent multitasker and made every second count. She was looking at something on her laptop, writing something on her legal pad, and looking at her tablet, all at the same time.

After a few minutes she looked up and said, "Every single

business day, I write five note cards to people who for one reason or another could possibly become a prospect. Not sure if
they will, but I'll never know until I make contact. Would you
please pick five business cards from the box and hand them to
me? I appreciate it."

Calvin didn't want to make a mistake with his first assignment. He pulled the small box toward him and looked inside. He
couldn't believe what he saw. There must have been 1,000 business cards stacked to the lid, each one with notes scribbled all
over the card.

Without thinking, Calvin opened his mouth and comment-
ed, "I don't know which ones to choose. Seems to me you would
want to pick the five that are most qualified, wouldn't you?"

Sarah smiled. "I don't mean to be rude, but you just broke
rules number 1 and 2. With all due respect, your job this week
isn't to think out loud or to ask questions before you've done
something I've requested. Simply do it. Thank you."

Calvin looked back down at the box. Wary of embarrassing
himself further, he reached down and took five cards with no
particular selection criteria in mind. "Here you go, Sarah. Didn't
mean to fail your first assignment."

"That's okay," Sarah said with a smile. "You aren't the first
rep who's done that, and you won't be the last. Now, I would
like you to read to me the name on the card, where they work,
and their title. Next please read the handwritten notes on the
card. The comments will say things like who gave me the referral and how they are related or fit with the solutions I provide.
Then, while I'm writing the note card, you can capture an image
of the business card with my smartphone. It will translate the
image into a contact in my suspect database. The only thing
you need to add is the name of the person who referred me.

Then set a reminder for me to send an e-mail to those contacts in five business days. Okay?"

Calvin agreed, pleased that he didn't say out loud what he was thinking. Why wasn't she just sending an e-mail to these referrals? That, it seemed to Calvin, *would be a lot simpler*.

Sarah interrupted his thoughts and said, "I'm ready for the first one. Whom do we have?"

Calvin looked at the five cards. *Which do I pick first?* he wondered silently. Something drew him to the second card on the left. He noticed the business title on the card: senior vice president. That seemed impressive enough.

Calvin read, "Bethany Stewart, senior VP at XYZ Corporation. Your notes say that she knows the manager at your dancing studio. Is that right?"

"Oh, yes, I remember the context. My husband and I are learning to ballroom dance at the local dance studio. The manager asked what I did and I told him. Just the other day he gave me that card you're holding and said he told Bethany about me, and she said to give her a call."

Calvin wanted to ask, *Is that all there is to it? Getting these referrals? Telling your dance instructor what you do and referrals fall from the sky onto the dance floor?*

Fortunately, he didn't. He simply took her smartphone, took a picture of the business card, logged her "to-do" in her calendar, and passed the card to Sarah, who clipped it to the note card she had just penned. Then she simply said, "Next!"

They performed that same procedure four more times, Sarah rhythmically going through the motions. It appeared to him that she was writing her note cards effortlessly. Curiously, she never paused to contemplate what she would write. She took each note card, and the ink began to flow.

When she finished writing the last card, she gave Calvin an appraising look. "You know, Calvin, I can tell you're a fast learner. Most of you new reps would have asked me which card to pick first or second out of the box. It's as though they are trying to determine which one has the best chance of becoming a new piece of business.

"The truth is, I've been doing this every day for almost four years, ever since I got here to this wonderful company. Here's what I've learned from doing this day in and day out for four years. It doesn't matter which card I do first or last. The point is to do something! Too many salespeople try to overthink how to get qualified prospects with the most efficiency, rather than trying to simply have enough people to speak with. There's a difference."

Calvin thought about what she had explained and said, "May I ask you one question?"

"Sure," she said, again with a smile. "What may I answer for you?"

"So tell me, Sarah," Calvin said, as sincerely as he could muster. "What is the one thing that I need to know so that I can have enough people to talk with? I'm guessing that one thing is one of the secrets of your success. Please forgive me for asking, but I humbly ask that you enlighten me."

"Flattery can only get you so far, but you do seem eager to learn!" Sarah quipped. "Okay, you want to know the one thing? Here it is—the one thing. The secret is simply this: One must earn one's referrals.

"Calvin, here's what I know," Sarah continued. "I'm not the smartest person or the funniest person or the most talented person in my job. I'd rank myself about average in brains and how-to. But what I do well is *sincerely serve people*. And that, over time, has made all the difference in the world for my business. Now, before we start talking too much theory, grab your keys. We have some appointments to make and you're driving!"

The rest of the day was a blur for Calvin. He had never witnessed anyone so fully engaged for eight full hours. She used every minute of the day talking with prospects, clients, coworkers, and peers on the phone, yet was always on time for her appointments, which seemed to be quick ones, never drawn out. She seemed as professional yet personable at the same time with everyone she encountered. At the end of the day, Sarah said she would meet him the next morning at the office at 8:30, just like this morning.

Calvin began to write down all the things he could remember Sarah doing that day that seemed different from anything he had done in his prior sales positions. After a few minutes he had several things on his list:

- Returns phone calls promptly
- Seems to ask everyone she speaks with, "What do you need?"
- Treats everyone the same, whether they're the SVP, their gatekeeper, or the server taking the lunch order
- Has the ability to really listen and repeat the words the person just said to her
- Everyone seems to ask for her advice

He looked at his list to see if he had missed anything. And then it came to him. With every person she encountered, she provided something of value to them, whether it was a kind word, a suggestion for a solution they were looking for, a name of someone who could help with a problem or concern they had, or as had happened twice today, two companies buying Sarah's products.

The next morning Calvin was 30 minutes early. Half of him was trying to impress his experienced colleague. The other half of him couldn't wait to ask her more questions. He headed straight for Conference Room B to join Sarah.

"Good morning, Sarah. I trust you had a good evening."

"I sure did, Calvin. And you?"

"Yes, I had a good evening. I must confess that I've been thinking about everything you said and what I learned yesterday."

"Well, Calvin, there will be plenty of time to talk about that. But first, we must repeat what we did yesterday. Pick five cards from the box."

As Calvin reached down, he glanced into the box and recognized two cards from yesterday's activities. "Hey, you put these cards from yesterday in the box. What determines whether a card is placed in the box or not?" It was an honest question that stumbled out without remembering rules number 1 or 2.

Sarah smiled but refused to answer. "Let's get our assignment done. Then I'll let you know."

Within 15 minutes Sarah had the five note cards completed. Calvin took pictures of the business cards. And just like yesterday, Sarah immediately had that rhythm. Before Calvin could finish his coffee, they were out the door for the second day.

CHAPTER 2

Common Language and Direct Value Statements

Throughout this book, we use some terms that are important for you to understand, and so, we are taking a few pages to define each. In a book like this, authors and readers should be on the same page, and we believe that a shared understanding of the specific terminology is a critical part of that agreement.

Connector: The source of a referral. This person provides you with the name and, ideally, an introduction to a potential source of business. For example, if you are selling website development services and a satisfied client refers you to his uncle's construction company, the satisfied client is your connector.

Referral: The person to whom the connector introduces you. This is the person who becomes a prospect. In the website developer example, your client's uncle is the referral.

Nonclient: A person or business that has not bought from you. Your list of nonclients includes everyone who might possibly buy from you, but has not yet done so. This might be a competitor of one of your current clients, for example.

Suspect: Someone to whom you would like to sell, but who has not yet expressed interest in your offering. If you attend a trade show, it is likely that most of the attendees are suspects.

Prospect: A person who is a slightly more interested suspect. In the trade show example again, the attendees who stop and visit your booth are prospects. See qualified prospect.

Qualified Prospect: Someone who has (1) a recognized need for your offering, (2) the ability and authority to buy from you, (3) a relative sense of urgency to buy what you sell, (4) a high level of trust in you or your organization, and (5) a willingness to listen to you.

Customer: A person or company that buys from you. Customers can be sources of referrals. For information on how to earn those referrals, refer to Part II of this book.

Client: A person or company with whom you have developed a professional, trust-based relationship. A client repeatedly buys from you. Clients are valuable sources of referrals because you have a deeper relationship with them than with your customers. For information on how to earn those referrals, refer to Part II of this book.

Zealot: A person who is so enthusiastic about you, your company, or your offering that he or she readily advocates on your behalf to potential referrals. This person becomes a connector who needs no prompting.

Perceived Benefits: The advantages that your prospect and/or customer believes he or she will receive by taking whatever action you are asking them to take. For example, if you buy a tablet computer, one perceived benefit is that you will be able to use it anywhere you go. We discuss perceived benefits in detail in Chapter 3.

Perceived Emotional Cost: The disadvantages that your prospect and/or customer believes he or she will face by taking whatever action you are asking them to take. For example, if you buy a tablet computer, one perceived emotional cost is the purchase price. Another is learning to use it. We discuss perceived emotional cost in detail in Chapter 3.

The Direct Value Statement

There is another term that is so important, it requires more than a simple definition: the **Direct Value Statement** (DVS). When you meet new connectors—or anyone for that matter—the way you describe the value you offer (the value you plan to ask a connector to refer to another, for example) determines whether you are referable. The most effective tool available to help you in this regard is the DVS.

To begin, what are the selling situations in which you find yourself most often? They can likely be broken into the following categories:

- Face-to-face, formally or informally
- By telephone
- At trade shows
- Through referrals from client connectors
- Through referrals from nonclient connectors
- At networking events
- Online

In each situation you need to know the importance and use of your own, one-of-a-kind DVS. Some people call this an *elevator speech*.

Whatever name you choose for the DVS, it's a straightforward, succinct statement that clearly and declaratively communicates the fundamental reason your organization exists and why you are selling its products or services. The concept of the DVS is probably the most important thing you will learn in this book, yet most salespeople never master the concept. Surprisingly, some have never even heard of it.

The purpose of the DVS is to quickly introduce what you can do for your clients in such a way that encourages the listener to say, "Tell me more." This gives you an opportunity to ask your audience some questions to determine whether they might serve as a qualified connector.

Sample Direct Value Statements

Throughout this chapter, you will notice two patterns common to an effective DVS, which should make crafting your DVS straightforward. The DVS is such an important concept that we spend some time showing you how to design your own.

Why is your DVS so important? Because it succinctly (there's that word again!), clearly, and precisely defines what you do and how you do it. Better yet, it defines clearly what you do and how you do it that would benefit your customers ... and identify your core customers. The DVS plays a central role in virtually every prospecting situation in which you will ever find yourself. In fact, this is explicit or implicit to it in every prospecting scenario explained in this book.

Here's one pattern you can try:

You say: I help X do Y so that Z. . . .

In that example, X represents the prospects you're after, Y is the action you take with them, and Z represents benefits they get. Let's take a look at some examples:

You say: I help women select their clothes so that they have more confidence.

You say: I help people who have been hurt in car accidents deal with the insurance companies so they get what they deserve.

You say: I help children get more exercise so that they live healthier lives.

You say: I help salespeople push their fears to the side so that they can have more of the professional successes they desire.

Here's another pattern you can try:

You say: We assist/help/serve clients (or customers) in the X industry (or business) to Y. We do this by Z.

Here's an example:

You say: We assist our clients in the banking industry to improve their profitability. We do this by reducing their costs, improving product performance, and geometrically expanding their markets.

No matter your business, your DVS can always start in the same way.

However, to do that, it's important for you to understand what benefits you deliver to your customers. You also need to know what benefits your prospects and customers want to gain, enjoy, achieve, or have.

Here are several examples:

You say: We assist our clients (or customers) in the interior design industry provide their clients a wide variety of cost-effective floor coverings. We do this by sourcing them directly from the manufacturer, which reduces our clients' costs.

You say: We assist our clients (or customers) studying for their real estate licenses to pass their state real estate exams easier, faster, and the first time. We do this by systematizing all the knowledge they need in a way that makes it easy to recall.

You say: We assist our clients (or customers) in the agriculture industry to get greater yields from their crops and enjoy greater profits. We do this by using the latest scientific methods and research.

You say: We help oral surgeons repair damaged teeth so their patients get their smiles back. We do this using the newest laser-driven technology.

You say: We help the family practice doctor experience more efficiency in the back office. We do this by providing the latest electronic medical records system that allows faster access to data.

You say: We help corporate aviation departments locate and procure the jet aircraft that meet their mission requirements. We do this by employing the world's largest database of new and used corporate aircraft.

You say: We serve our customers creative lunches and dinners that appeal to their desire to eat in a more health-conscious way. We do this by substituting flavorful, healthy ingredients for higher calorie options.

You say: We assist our small business customers in the professional services industry become more technologically advanced to better serve their clients. We do this by providing them with technology that is typically available only to the Fortune 500.

Using the Direct Value Statement

Your DVS is critical. As you'll see, you can use it to gain appointments with connectors, meet new people, answer the question, "What do you do?" and in lots of other situations.

This structure resembles the DVS we just introduced::

You say: We assist/help/serve our W in the X industry to Y. We do this by Z.

No matter what your business, venture, service, or industry, this statement will work for you. We urge you to give serious thought to answering these four questions when developing your own DVS:

1. Do you work with individuals, organizations, enterprises, associations, or governments?
2. Do you specialize in an industry? Market? Type of business?
3. What do you help your customers do? Reduce costs? Improve productivity? Reduce turnover? Maximize returns? Gain market share? Enhance stock value? Improve profits?
4. How do you do that? By improving processes? Improving manufacturing yield? Providing upgraded equipment?

If you cannot communicate the fundamental reason people or organizations choose to do business with you and how you do what you do, you will have a serious problem prospecting for customers. In fact, if you can't verbalize those things, you will likely never even get your foot in the door.

In the final analysis, people choose to refer you if they believe you can help their referral reduce or remove a problem, solve an issue, improve a situation, or enhance their positions. They are vitally interested in securing solutions. That's really what it's all about. As a result, your DVS must communicate that idea.

Here are some more examples:

You say: We assist our clients (or customers) in the communication industry reduce personnel costs. We do this by offering screening and assessment services, hiring systems, and retention programs.

You say: We assist veterinarians in rural markets provide better care to large farm animals. We do this by having the largest research facility in the world with more scientists dedicated solely to large animal care.

You say: We help elementary school teachers provide real-time experiences for their students. We do this by offering more than 300 real-world learning products at discount prices that we market through home parties for teachers, sponsored by teachers.

You say: We provide great-tasting, fast-serve breakfast sandwiches for our customers so they have more productive mornings. We do this by building a large network of easy-to-find restaurants.

You say: We help our distributors of outdoor textiles deliver on-target solutions for their customers. We do this by manufacturing the highest quality, largest selection of outdoor fabrics in the industry.

You say: We help our clients ensure their warehouses are hazard free. We do this by teaching them how to use the safest forklifts ever produced.

Your turn. Fill in the blanks of your value statement.

You say: We assist/help/serve W [customers] in X [industry or occupation] to Y [how you help]. We do this by Z [your solution].

Of all the things explained in this book, this one concept could be the most important to your sales career. Craft your DVS and use it over and over. It will be invaluable to you in gaining appointments with even the most difficult prospects.

More than any other statement in this book, you must deliver your DVS with ease and confidence. In fact, ideally you should be able to recite it as comfortably as you tell someone your name.

Again, the DVS is one of the most powerful tools available to you when building relationships, especially with nonclient connectors. The better job you do in capturing their attention, the better job you can do explaining the value you offer to the people they can then refer you to.

PART

PERFECT PHRASES FOR
CLIENT-GENERATED
REFERRALS

CHAPTER 3

What Keeps People from Earning Referrals

Before you take steps to grow your referral opportunities, it's important to explore the common reasons we've seen salespeople resist the advice to ask for referrals. The explanations all relate to negative beliefs. Reversing those negative beliefs begins with a process of positive self-talk. There are 12 common reasons salespeople fail to earn referrals. Through the years, we have noticed that these stumbling blocks are easy to overcome if a salesperson is willing to admit his or her shortcomings. Let's take a look at them.

12 Reasons You Don't Earn Referrals

1. You Aren't Following Up on the Referrals You're Getting

Believe it or not, some salespeople don't follow up on the referrals they're already receiving. Sometimes they make this mistake because they decide the referral is weak. Other times it's because of a sense that they should only spend their efforts on new opportunities. Regardless of the salesperson's "excuse," the real reason is probably poor time management. We discuss time management later in this chapter.

Failing to follow up on referrals is an amateur sales mistake that should be avoided at all costs. If you receive a referral, treat it like gold, because that is exactly what it might put into your pocket.

2. You're Asking the Wrong People

It's possible that you're asking the wrong people. For example, if you're selling medical devices, it probably doesn't make a lot of sense to network with accounting professors (unless they specialize in medical practice accounting). But the mistake can be more subtle than that. A qualified connector has four characteristics:

a. They have received value from you.
b. They trust and/or respect you.
c. They understand who your target audience is and have connections to it.
d. They believe in the value you can offer to the target audience.

In Chapter 4, we provide you with more details about the four characteristics of a qualified connector. For now, keep in mind that you should focus your efforts only on the most qualified connectors.

We also provide the specific phrases to use so that you're given qualified referrals. The quick takeaway is that if the people you're asking for referrals don't know people for whom you can provide value, it probably doesn't make sense for you to invest your referral-hunting time with them.

3. You Aren't Successfully Explaining Your Value

Another reason you might not be earning referrals is because you're not doing a good job of explaining what you do. You must be able to describe the value you offer to people or companies in a way that captures the attention of your audience. Further, your description must be easily translatable by your audience to someone else so they can tell their referrals about you. Remember the Direct Value Statement in Chapter 2? Your DVS has to immediately build value. For example, which is more referable?

You hear: What do you do?

You say: I'm in sales for a research company.

You hear: What do you do?

You say: I work with life science companies that need specific information about their target clients. I help them uncover that information so they close deals faster. We do this by aiming our proprietary search technology at the Deep Web. Together, we identify factors like how long their target prospect has been working there, where they went to college, and other useful facts.

When you read that DVS it may or may not make sense to you. If it does, you're probably a target for this salesperson. If it doesn't, he or she hasn't done a good job of tailoring it to you.

4. You're Not Laying the Groundwork

This is the most obvious blunder referral-seeking salespeople make: They don't ask. One of the basic tenets of sales is that "You can't win a sale you don't ask for." Unfortunately, according to one study, 62 percent of salespeople fail to ask for a sale. The same mistake applies to seeking referrals.

If you're providing value and earning trust, but aren't laying the groundwork to later earn a referral, you're making a common but easily remedied mistake. We provide many valuable phrases to lay the groundwork to earn referrals throughout the book, but here's a quick suggestion:

You say: Please don't keep me a secret. If you've found value in the services/products I provide, I hope you'll share your experience with others.

5. You Use the "Wrong" Language

Using the right language for the right referral source is critical.

Are you using too many industry terms or too much slang? Or not enough? The right answer depends on whom you're meeting with. If you're speaking with a referral source who is unfamiliar with your industry, but might be able to introduce you to prospective clients, don't overuse confusing terms. Acronyms and technical terms are off-putting and distracting to some potential referral sources. Using those technical terms can lead someone who doesn't know them to feel lost. Put bluntly: Someone who's made to feel overwhelmed or confused is unlikely to provide you with a referral because they can't understand your value.

If, on the other hand, you're speaking to a prospective referral source and fail to use the proper technical terms that they know and understand, you're setting yourself up for failure.

Looking credible to a referral source is essential—it's how you build trust. If you fail to establish yourself as an expert in your field, it's less likely that you'll earn referrals.

6. You Have Poor Follow-Through

Still another reason you might not be earning referrals is because you're failing to provide exceptional follow-through with your existing customers. If you're looking for referrals from existing clients, there's a simple strategy to follow: After winning a sale, service the account beyond any reasonable expectation. At that point, you can be confident in your efforts to seek referrals. In essence, you're earning those referrals by providing greater-than-expected value. You can test this by asking yourself one of these questions and responding with an honest yes or no.

You ask yourself: Have I exceeded every reasonable expectation this customer/client could have relative to service?

You ask yourself: Has each and every request made by this customer/client been dealt with fairly and professionally?

You ask yourself: Is this customer/client overwhelmingly satisfied with everything we've provided them?

7. You Don't Believe In or Understand Your Offering

Salespeople sometimes fail to earn referrals because they don't believe in (or understand) their offering. If you don't have a fundamental belief in the product or service you're selling, we suggest you do some serious soul searching.

Gain confidence in your product or service by studying it and its impact on your customers. Use these affirmations to promote your positive beliefs about your product.

You tell yourself: Without my product/service, my clients would not be as successful as they need to be.

You tell yourself: My product/service allows my customers to bring value to their customers.

8. You Aren't Adapting to the Connector's Personality

Personality conflicts are a leading killer of sales interactions. Our clients observe field salespeople and provide curbside coaching. Recently, we observed one struggling salesperson. He showed promise early in his career, but his success waned. Within the first 30 seconds, we saw the problem. He failed to modify his behavior to his prospect. He was overbearing. Here's part of the transcript of the actual interaction our consultant observed.

He heard: Hi.

He said: Hiya! How are you? I'm so glad to meet with you. Can you believe how hot it is out there? [long pause]. Okay. So, when you're not working, what do you like to do?

He heard: I work a lot.

He said: I hear you. I love to get on my boat. You?

He heard: [Salesperson starts speaking, but client interrupts]

He said: Well, anyway, is that a picture of your wife? She's really pretty. You're a lucky man.

It was an unbelievable blind spot. The salesperson simply didn't see how his personality was overwhelming his customers. Obviously, our coaching aimed to help him adapt to his prospect. Beyond the initial botched sales interaction, a salesperson with that kind of demeanor is not referable.

You must also adapt to a connector when you're seeking a referral. Instead of adopting the old-school, glad-handing style, approach in neutral, adjust your energy level up or down depending on the connector's personality and avoid unso-licited small talk.

9. You Suffer from Self-Deprecation

Another reason salespeople resist referrals is that they don't believe their status is equal to their prospect's. This self-depre-cating attitude is a like a virus. Once it starts, it's hard to fight. One of the most interesting ways companies combat this sense of inadequacy is by changing their sales team's job titles to something like Strategic Partner Advisor or Business Strategy Consultant. In truth, no job title will overcome a lack of intrinsic belief in one's own abilities. Improve your sense of self by prac-ticing positive self-talk. It's critical to believe in yourself and your ability to provide value to your prospects. Use these phrases to promote your positive beliefs about yourself.

You tell yourself: I am a capable, confident, professional sales-person.

You tell yourself: I create great value for my customers.

You tell yourself: Without me, my customers' most important needs, wants, and desires could never be satisfied.

You tell yourself: The value I create for my customers is worth far more than I ask them to pay for it.

10. You Believe Your Clients Won't Give Referrals

Another reason for this resistance to asking for referrals is that some salespeople believe their customers won't give them referrals because of a fear of helping the competition. This is really a reflection of a failure to first build value. If you have cre-ated a high level of value for your client and nonclient connec-tors, they will freely and gladly provide you referrals. Even connectors who don't want to introduce you to their direct competitors can connect you with referrals in other regions or industries.

You think you'll hear: I don't want to share you with my competitors. It'll put me out of business.

You tell yourself: I've provided such vast amounts of value that no one would retreat from the opportunity to provide equivalent value to me.

11. You Only Want to Talk to Prospects

Some salespeople resist asking for referrals because they believe talking to anyone other than a real, live, going-to-close-soon prospect is a waste of time. Nothing could be further from the truth. By carefully identifying qualified client and nonclient connectors the same way you carefully identify qualified prospects, you can benefit from the flow of the *river of referrals*.

Repeat this statement to help yourself understand the benefits of speaking with qualified connectors.

You tell yourself: The time I invest with qualified connectors is essential if I'm going to create rivers of referrals flowing to my office.

12. You're an Approval Seeker

If you're fundamentally an approval seeker, you're setting yourself up for failure. Are you willing to say anything you can to get your prospective referral sources to like you? If you are, you will be just another face in the crowd. When we ask business-to-business (B2B) prospects what they think of interactions with salespeople, we hear all kinds of reactions. Here's a typical response:

We asked: When a salesperson is about to meet with you—in person or by phone—what goes through your mind?

We heard: I know that they'll start with small talk about the weather, traffic, or hobbies we might have in common. Then, when they think I like them, they'll slide right into sales talk. To be honest with you, I don't like it—or them. I don't care whether we share hobbies. Let's just get down to business.

That's no way to earn referrals. In short, the glib, glad-handing, approval-seeking, overly positive salespeople just don't earn enough trust to warrant referrals. To build a river of referrals, you have to be different. You must learn about the Give-to-Get. It's our philosophy of referrals, which we explore in Chapter 4.

The *Real* Reasons for Lack of Referrals

With that said, we want to share a secret with you. For 35 years, The Brooks Group has been in the business of observing, coaching, training, and improving sales organizations. Sure, we've seen each of the 12 reasons above. But we've also seen something else that's surprising.

We've learned that the 12 reasons you don't get referrals boil down to three overriding causes. In essence, the connectors you're dealing with don't feel that you have (1) earned their trust, (2) provided them with value, or (3) displayed confidence. Let's take a look at each one.

Insufficient Trust

Recently we scientifically quantified how quickly trust is earned. Only a few years ago, two Princeton psychologists, Janine Willis and Alexander Todorov, conducted a study in which they determined that people decide whether they trust each other within the first one tenth of a second of meeting.

The researchers flashed photographs of people's faces in front of participants and asked them to say whether they found the people in the photos trustworthy. Regardless of whether the photo was in front of the viewers for a microsecond or for as long as the study participant wished, the results were the same: People determined how much they trusted the people in those photographs within the first one tenth of a second.

We're not telling you that you only have one tenth of a second to develop trust. We are saying that's where your first impression begins. Following the first impression, it's possible to do a lot to increase your trust level and the likelihood of earning a referral. The phrases in this book have been carefully researched, studied, and tested to build trust. However, it's important to recognize that trust alone is insufficient. You must also work to generate value.

Insufficient Value

The best way to earn the right to receive referrals is to overwhelm a potential connector with value. In Chapter 5, we go into detail about how you can increase the number of earned referrals by providing value to the right people. There's no way around it: The best route to a river of referrals is by earning them.

But what is value?

$$\text{Value} = \frac{\text{Perceived benefits (what they will get by working with you)}}{\text{Perceived emotional cost (what working with you costs them)}}$$

Value is a formula. *Perceived benefits* are those things that a connector has received from you as a result of working with you. They might include a high level of service for existing clients or even referrals that you've provided them. The perceived benefits also include the goodwill and the opportunity to help someone else by providing you with a referral. Other perceived benefits might include the opportunity to qualify for a discount or some kind of corporate referral program.

The most significant *perceived emotional costs* of providing a referral includes putting one's reputation at risk. Other perceived emotional costs a connector might consider include providing a referral that a salesperson never follows up on or even referring someone to a poor product or service. You must overcome the perceived emotional costs by providing value before earning a referral.

Put simply, the higher the benefits and the lower the emotional costs, the more likely it is that you'll receive a referral.

In the following chapters, we discuss our Give-to-Get (G2G) philosophy. Suffice it to say, the more value you provide to a connector, the more likely it is that he or she will provide you with referral opportunities.

So, if you're doing a good job of building trust and value, surely earning referrals should be easy, right? Unfortunately, the short answer is maybe.

Insufficient Confidence

You'll never earn referrals if you don't believe in your profession, your industry, your company, and your product. There are two things that will hold you back more than anything else—your lack of self-confidence and lack of belief in yourself. If you don't believe you deserve to get referrals, it won't happen.

You must defeat negative self-talk. Some salespeople roll their eyes at the idea of positive affirmations or motivation, but we believe they can be some of the most powerful phrases in your sales vocabulary.

If you believe: I'm not worthy of success. I won't ever be wealthy, then ...

Tell yourself: I am a capable, confident, professional salesperson.

Tell yourself: I deserve to be successful.

Tell yourself: I achieve my goals and I am fulfilled by what I do.

If you believe: Sales is not a highly regarded profession, then ...

Tell yourself: Sales is an honorable profession worthy of my best efforts.

Tell yourself: Sales is a profession that allows me to create great value for my customers.

Tell yourself: Without me, my customers' most important needs, wants, and desires could never be satisfied.

If you believe: My industry is a joke,* then ...

Tell yourself: The role we play in society is critical to our customers and the people who work in my company.

Tell yourself: We are an essential part of the economy.

Tell yourself: It's because of my sales that many families have food on their tables tonight.

If you believe: My product/service is worthless,* then ...

Tell yourself: My product/service is worth a lot more than I ask my prospects and customers to pay for it.

Tell yourself: My product/service is invaluable to my prospects and customers.

Tell yourself: In the absence of my product/service, my prospects or clients would not be as successful as they need to be.

If you believe: My employer doesn't deliver value to our customers,* then ...

---

* If you believe these statements, you should carefully consider whether your current role is right for you.

Tell yourself: My company and I work hard to ensure we always promise a lot and deliver more.

Tell yourself: My company is well respected and delivers even more than it promises.

Tell yourself: My employer is the best in the industry.

Tip: Select four or five of those affirmations and place each one on a card that you can look at every day. When you see it, repeat each one up to 30 times in 30 days. You'll be surprised at how well that works to change your mindset.

Improve Your Time Management

There's one more factor that might be causing you to struggle to earn referrals. That challenge is effective time management.

There's a chance that you're caught up in activities that, while they may be productive, do not contribute to earning referrals. This is a big problem most salespeople face. The very people who are attracted to the fast-paced nature of sales careers are often those least fit to effectively manage their time. The best time managers have three things going for them:

1. An understanding of the value of time
2. An understanding of the specific tools and skills of time management
3. Practice in using the tools and skills of time management

Understanding the Value of Time

The first step toward understanding the value of your time and where it can go is to consider the ways you spend your time. We use a tool called the *time analysis grid* to demonstrate this concept (Figure 3-1).

Ideally, you will spend more time achieving your targeted accomplishments (cell 1 of the grid). Another significant boost

Figure 3-1. Time analysis grid

to your overall effectiveness will come from meeting the challenges posed by firefighting (cell 2). Additional major gains in your ability to get control of your time will come from eliminating the need to spend time on other people's priorities (cell 3) and time-wasters (cell 4).

Time-wasters (cell 4) come in many forms. One of the best examples is chasing unqualified connectors. However, others include telephone interruptions, drop-in visitors, procrastination, waiting for meetings to start, hopping from project to project, and doing low-priority activities simply because they are easy or pleasant. Avoid these time-wasters by being honest with yourself when one of them is creeping into your day. Stomp it out!

You say: My time is my most valuable asset.

You say: I will not waste my time on the trivial.

You say: I will not put off until tomorrow what I can do right now.

Other people's priorities (cell 3) present a dilemma. On one hand, cooperation and teamwork are the hallmarks of effective management and corporate etiquette. On the other hand, always helping others achieve their priorities at the sacrifice of your own goals is self-destructive. Avoid these potholes by respectfully guarding your time.

You say: I appreciate the fact that you need me to help with this. Unfortunately, I'm busy with other projects.

You say: I wish I could help you; however, my plate is full with other commitments.

You say: Thank you for thinking of me, and it would be great to help you on that. Unfortunately, we're getting near the end of the quarter, and my time has to be spent earning more business.

Learning to manage your activities effectively enough to avoid the need to spend your time fighting fires (cell 2) is a significant challenge. For many of us, learning to live without fighting fires means breaking lifelong habits. However, mastery of skills like problem solving, decision making, and delegation provide most of the tools necessary to prevent crisis management. Unfortunately, an in-depth discussion of these topics is beyond the scope of this book.

You say: I will plan more effectively to avoid surprises.

You say: I will avoid emergencies by working smarter.

Targeted accomplishment (cell 1) results from establishing priorities, setting goals, identifying milestones, and meeting those deadlines. Most of your day should be devoted to planned activities of high importance. This also allows you to link your daily to-do list to your major goals. Here's an example:

■ **Establish Priorities:** Within the next year, 85 percent of my new business will come from referrals.

- **Set Goals:** Within one week of earning the right to do so by providing value, I will ask every qualified connector for referrals.
- **Identify Milestones:** After (date), each meeting with a qualified prospect will have come from a referral.
- **To Do:** Check with each of my customers from last week to determine their satisfaction. If appropriate, I will ask for referrals.

Leverage Your Tools

Every potential time-wasting tool can also be used to generate more referrals.

After meeting with tens of thousands of salespeople, we have discovered that the least leveraged tool is e-mail. We suggest that if you have more than eight e-mails in your inbox at any one time, you're wasting time. All e-mail falls into one of four categories:

1. Delete: If it's junk or spam, delete it.
2. Delegate: If someone else can or should handle it, pass it along.
3. File: If it's simply for your review, file it in an appropriate folder.
4. Respond: If your reaction is necessary, respond within 24 hours.

That's it! We've seen inboxes that literally have thousands of unread e-mails in them. How likely is it that a qualified connector will happily provide you with referrals if they're never followed up on because they're lost in your inbox? The answer is simple: Not very. We explore this concept in Chapter 8 by giving you specific phrases to use when writing referral-generating e-mails.

Another popular time-consuming tool is social media. If you're honest with yourself, how much of your time is spent on social media sites? If you're not using that time to generate referrals, you'd better stop. To use social media more effectively, remind your friends and followers of what you do and how you can help them and their contacts. Do this by sharing on social media (Facebook, Twitter, etc.) the value you've been bringing to your customers.

You post: Because of the tools and systems we provide, I just helped a business owner save 15 percent!

You tweet: Due to our product, our company is helping businesses increase revenues by 27 percent!

We talk more about how to use social media as a referral generator throughout the book, but the take-away here is that you should look at those time-wasting tools as referral opportunities.

Moving beyond the tools, it's important to really understand your time. The best way to do that is by keeping a time-use log. As old-school as this sounds, it can truly be an eye-opener into your activities. Marking what you're doing in 15-minute blocks will reveal tremendous opportunities to open up new time for you to invest in referral-generating activities.

Give-to-Get Meets Time Management

Given the pressure you're under to maximize every moment of your time, it's clear how important it is to spend time in the most referral-rich places. To truly take advantage of the G2G philosophy, it's important to consider how you are perceived by potential nonclient connectors who can refer you to new opportunities.

First, looking for potential nonclient connectors is one of the "hardest easy things" you'll do. Why is that? Because they are everywhere. Narrow it down with a question like this:

Ask Yourself: Who, like me, will benefit from relationships with the kinds of people I'd like to sell to? Where do they spend time?

You might also consider this question:

Ask Yourself: Who are the people who, if you knew them, could catapult your business to the next level?

Once you have a sense of who those people are, seek them out. The answer to the question ("Who are these people?") will give you a good idea of where to spend your time prospecting for connectors. You might find some of them at/in/on:

- Clubs and organizations
- Chamber of Commerce
- Nonprofit boards of directors
- Religious organizations
- Economic development organizations
- Industry associations

What you are trying to do is find people to network with. Seek out noncompeting businesses or salespeople who also sell to your target clients. There is an excellent chance that you will be able to share opportunities with one another.

Noncompetitive Groups

A great example comes from Paul, an industrious salesperson working for one of our clients in the courier industry. Paul sells courier services to small and midsized businesses. One day, he received a call from the managing partner at a law firm resulting from a referral by a friend of Paul's who sold office furniture. He recognized an opportunity. He reached out to that connector and asked her to join him for a cup of coffee. The two realized they were on to something: *why not create a group of noncompeting salespeople who sold to law firms?*

They did it. Included in the group were:

- Paul, who sold courier services
- Janette, who sold office furniture
- Steve, who sold office electronics
- Gary, who sold IT consulting services
- Sally, who sold legal research services
- Phil, who represented a company offering mediation and transcription services

None of them competed, and they shared opportunities with one another. For Paul, it turned a great prospecting tool into a profitable business segment he had not previously considered.

The challenge is obvious: How do you isolate the good potential connectors from the bad ones? How do you know whom to invite into your group?

We mentioned the four characteristics of a qualified connector earlier and we discuss them in depth in Chapter 4, but they bear repeating:

1. They have received value from you.
2. They trust and/or respect you.
3. They understand who your target audience is and have connections to it.
4. They believe in the value you can offer to the target audience.

Self-Assessment

Use this self-assessment to determine how effective you are at earning referrals. By completing this assessment, you will know where you stand when it comes to your overall "referability." It will help you see how to take the information in this book and use it in your daily sales efforts.

Use a 1–7 scale: 1 = 0% of the time; 2 = 20% of the time; 3 = 30% of the time; 4 = 50% of the time; 5 = 70% of the time; 6 = 80% of the time; 7 = 100% of the time

__ I seek to develop trust with my business associates before trying to get them to like me.
__ I adapt my language to the people I'm meeting with rather than memorizing a script.
__ I adapt my energy level and personal presentation to help my business associates feel comfortable.
__ I feel confident asking for referrals.
__ When I ask for referrals, I get them.
__ My new opportunities come from referrals.

__ I only ask a customer for referrals after they've used my product or service.

__ I feel I deserve to receive referrals from people.

__ I feel my company deserves to receive referrals.

__ I believe that what I sell brings great value to the people who buy it.

__ I am invited by customers to provide my expertise even when no sale is pending.

__ When I get a new opportunity, I'm the only salesperson trying to earn the business.

__ I look for opportunities to offer referrals to others.

__ I provide referrals to others when the opportunity arises.

__ I receive unexpected referrals.

__ When I receive a referral, I follow up on it within a reasonable time.

__ I am careful about whom I ask for referrals.

__ I can answer every question a customer asks me about my product/service.

__ I can answer every question a customer asks me about my industry.

__ I can answer every question a customer asks me about my other customers' businesses (that are not confidential).

__ There is no way I could provide any more value to my customers than I already do.

Total your points from each answer.

- 122–147: Great work, those referrals must be flooding in!
- 97–121: You're getting there. Just a bit more work to do.
- 72–96: Impressive, but there's still more you can do.
- 47–71: You have some work to do.
- 21–46: This is an opportunity to improve. Use the strategies in this book to really have some impact!

Conclusion

So to determine where you stand when it comes to your likelihood of earning referrals, begin by focusing on delivering trust and value with confidence to your connectors. Then, ensure that you aren't making any of the common mistakes salespeople make that fail to earn them referrals. Finally, ensure you're exercising good time management.

CHAPTER 4

Give-to-Get

Do not impose on others what you yourself do not desire.
— Confucius

Our research has shown that the best way to generate rivers of referrals is to use the Give-to-Get, or G2G, approach. It involves two simple tasks. First, you give something of value to the referral-giver before asking for anything in return. Second, you provide the referral-giver with emotional triggers so that he or she can easily contact you to provide specific, qualified referrals. It really is as simple as that.

Remember Sarah from Chapter 1? When Calvin asked her to identify the one thing a salesperson must know to find enough people to talk with, Sarah responded, "Here it is—the one thing. The secret is simply this: *one must earn one's referrals.*"

We cover a number of specific strategies to give value to potential referral-givers. We also teach you precise emotional words to use to elicit immediate recall and delivery of qualified referrals.

Stop Stumbling on Referrals

As a result of our sales training work, we have the opportunity to speak with thousands of salespeople each year. When we ask what they think of referrals,

We hear: Sure! Referrals are an important part of my prospecting efforts. They're the best source of business.

But, when we press those same salespeople about how they're actively seeking referrals,

We hear something else: Well, I guess they just come when they come. I don't ask for them. That's too risky.

That response is all too common. So many salespeople lack a consistent approach to referrals. And, because they don't do it systematically, they are afraid to ask for them. Stop stumbling on referrals. Instead, look at earning referrals as an important part of your daily activities.

A referral-generating business does not happen by accident. It's a systematic approach that begins with providing excellent service and a few key phrases.

A Referral Philosophy

The most successful way to get referrals is to earn them. The foundational philosophy of this book is called Give-to-Get. In essence, by giving value, you get it in return. Of course, you must connect to get connected. Throughout this book, we provide the phrases to use to make those connections that allow you to Give-to-Get referrals.

By adopting the G2G philosophy, you need to acknowledge that the best way to get referrals is to truly believe that the only way to get them is to earn them. You must provide (give) something of value before expecting referrals to be provided (get).

A great example of the G2G philosophy at work is giving a free sample. Consider a discount warehouse store. Often, while walking through those stores, you can get a free sample of their bulk goods. Why? They do it, in part, to expose you to those goods, but also because, by providing those samples, they are triggering the law of reciprocation. Think back to the last time you wandered the halls of one of those warehouses, were offered a sample of something, and then bought it (even if you didn't really want it). That's G2G at work.

Another example comes from your friends. Remember the last time you received help from a friend. When you did, you no doubt felt some obligation to return the favor. In other words, your friend would not have earned the favor without first doing something for you. By providing value to you, he received a return.

If you'd like to test the G2G principle, offer a sincere compliment to someone. There is a good chance that your compliment will be reciprocated. It's human nature.

In his book *Influence*, Dr. Robert Cialdini wrote about the law of reciprocation, a close relative of the principle of G2G. He said that reciprocation is based on the idea that "we should try to repay, in kind, what another person has provided us." When you receive a favor, you're likely to feel the need to repay it.

The Golden Rule, international political alliances, business partnerships, and even marriages are built on the G2G principle. It is ingrained into the very fabric of our society. And for that reason, the G2G philosophy can be easily applied to earning referrals. G2G works whether you're hoping to earn client-generated referrals or even nonclient-generated referrals. If you serve someone, regardless of whether they've bought something from you, it is only natural for them to serve you back. Now, let's take a look at some ways you can serve. We share a few trigger phrases to introduce the concepts to you, but we go into detail in later chapters.

As a professional salesperson, you must adopt the attitude that "In order to get, I must give." This isn't always a natural approach for salespeople, and we recommend repeating an affirmation to yourself.

You say: To earn rivers of referrals, I must provide abundant value to those around me.

You say: I will seek opportunities to provide others with value before expecting it to be returned to me.

You say: I will most likely get referrals if I first give value. But I will never get referrals if I haven't first given value.

Put yourself in the shoes of a connector for a moment. You've been asked to provide a referral to a salesperson to help him. As a connector, here's what's probably going through your mind:

The connector thinks: If I provide this referral, I'm putting my reputation on the line. I'm making a recommendation to my friend/coworker/colleague/family member. Is this endorsement really worth it? What if the product or service doesn't work right? What if this guy never follows up with the person I'm referring to him? What if this salesperson rips my friend off? What if ...

Our point is simple: When you ask for a referral, you're asking a lot more from the connector than just a name. This is why the old-school sales tactic of asking anyone who breathes for a referral is a mistake. At worst, you lose credibility. At best, you get someone's name who may, or more likely may not, be a good lead. The reason is clear: if a connector hasn't received value from you, she's unlikely to connect you with her most prized connections. And she's certainly unlikely to provide you with the Midas touch of referrals—a solid introduction.

The only way to overcome the connector's concerns is to adopt the G2G philosophy. You must give value to get referrals. It's as simple as that. Of course, you can provide more value than anyone in your industry, but if you do not actually ask for referrals, you will only receive a small percentage of the possibilities that exist.

Knowing Whom to Ask: The Four Characteristics of a Qualified Connector

Of course, it's essential to serve your connectors before they'll be willing to provide you with referrals. However, it's also essential that you carefully select the best connectors to serve. The key to selling is to be in front of a prospective customer when he or she is ready to buy, not when you need to make a sale. This concept can also be applied to earning referrals: The secret to selling is to be in front of a qualified connector when he or she is ready to recommend you to a new opportunity, not when you need to earn a referral.

Not everyone is a great connector. Why? Because not everyone fulfills the characteristics of a qualified connector.

All of the best connectors have four things in common:

1. They have received value from you.
2. They trust and/or respect you (whether this is earned or "just a feeling").
3. They understand who your target audience is and have connections to it.
4. They believe in the value you can offer to the target audience.

They Have Received Value from You

Connectors who have experienced or are aware of a high level of service from you are likely to be able to share your successes with others. But being able to share your successes is far different from actually promoting you. And, because those zealots are few and far between, you've got to help them share your story with the people you're seeking.

The first step in identifying whether a potential client connector will be a good one for you is to determine his level of satisfaction with your work so far.

If you're new to a territory or are new to sales and don't have a pool of satisfied customers, you can still find good connectors. Do this by offering value to the people who you determine could be good connectors. For example, provide referrals to them.

Here are a few examples of ways to determine if a potential connector is satisfied:

You ask: How would you describe your experience with our company so far?

You hear: Everything has been great. I've been really impressed by your on-time delivery. It's a lot better than our previous supplier.

You ask: When we first began meeting, you contacted our company because you [faced some problem, challenge, etc.]. How would you describe our work together to a friend in a similar situation?

You hear: I guess I'd tell them that you've helped sort out the situation and made us a lot more profitable. I'd probably tell them about the fact that you have a lot of industry knowledge and predicted the [problem, challenge, etc.] before we encountered it.

You ask: What would you say are the reasons you have remained with us?

You hear: I'm consistently impressed by how great your customer service is. Whenever we have a problem, we call up, and it's solved pretty quickly.

Identifying effective connectors with whom to build referral-based relationships is a critical step. Asking the wrong people for referrals will almost guarantee failure.

It's always better to ask prospective connectors specific questions. Asking someone something as broad as "Whom do you know?" is unlikely to generate much response. That's because the narrower the range is, the more accurate the response is. Here's an example:

You ask: As you'll recall, we originally met because you were struggling with maintaining your inventory. Whom do you know who's facing a similar challenge today?

You hear: Jane, a long-time friend of mine over at Moody, Inc., recently said she was having that problem, too. I should have mentioned you to her.

You say: That's all right. Do you think it would be all right for me to contact Jane?

You hear: Sure.

You say: May I use your name when I do?

You hear: Absolutely.

They Trust and/or Respect You

As stated in Chapter 1, all you really sell are *trust* and *value*. The same is true of connectors. If they trust you, they're more likely to risk their reputations by referring their connections to you.

Earning trust and/or respect is all about showcasing your credibility. You will not be referred without establishing confidence in your abilities in the minds of connectors. Think about it: Why would you refer someone other than the most highly competent person to your friends, family, and colleagues? The answer is that you wouldn't. To be referable, you must be perceived as having a high level of expertise.

To test whether someone trusts you, listen for phrases like this:

You hear: I feel like we can discuss just about anything.

You hear: I really appreciate the direction of our discussions.

You hear: Do you mind if I ask you a question that's not related to business?

Another way to establish your credibility is to get published. Write an article for an industry publication and gain instant authority. Even better, publish a book or speak on your topic. When that happens, you earn a new level of believability.

Understanding—and Connecting to—Your Audience

If your connector doesn't know or understand who your target audience is, you need to explain it to him.

You say: Who is your ideal client?

You hear: [A description of his ideal client]

You say: That's interesting. Do you know [someone or some company that falls into that category]?

You hear: No, I don't.

You say: Well, let me make an introduction.

You hear: That would be great!

You say: Wonderful. You know, I'm not sure whether I've ever explained my ideal client to you.

You hear: No, I don't think you have. Please do.

You say: We work with companies of 15 to 50 employees that don't have their own IT department. We help them by addressing all their IT needs while at the same time keeping their costs really low.

Believe in Your Value

The right connectors have strong beliefs in the value that you have to offer. You must ensure that they have firm beliefs that what you have to offer is valuable for the people they might introduce you to. If they don't believe in your value, it's unlikely they will place their reputations on the line by recommending that people consider your products or services. Measure this by asking feedback questions:

You say: Do you see how this might benefit anyone you know?

You say: Does this appear to be something that you would feel comfortable recommending to friends?

You say: Can you see this working for others?

You say: How do you think your [coworkers, family, friends] might feel about this?

You say: Might this be helpful to anyone else?

Leveraging Relationships

Beyond knowing whether a connector has the four characteristics to be considered qualified, you must also understand how you can leverage your relationship with her. To leverage your relationship, you need to do some planning before meeting with the potential connector. Even if you're meeting with a long-term client or old friend, you will be well served to prepare.

Here's some of the information you should learn before meeting:

■ Where does this connector work?
■ How do you know this connector?
■ What mutual contacts do I share with this connector?
■ What social media profiles exist (e.g., LinkedIn, Twitter, YouTube) that might provide some information about this

person and/or her company?

- How close is your relationship with this connector?
- How much experience does this connector have with you?
- How much experience does this connector have with your product?
- How much experience does this connector have with your company?
- How much experience does this connector have with your industry?
- Where is this connector placed inside her current company?
- What industry is this connector in?
- To whom would you like this connector to introduce you?
- To whom might this connector be likely to introduce you?
- Who else might be asking this connector for referrals?
- What experience does this connector have with giving and/or receiving referrals?
- How does this connector prefer to communicate?
- What would it look like to earn a referral from this connector? Will she be an action-oriented connector (making introductions for you) or a permission-oriented connector (providing you with names to reach out to on her behalf)?

Naturally, it isn't possible to have all this information before meeting to request referrals, but just as in sales, the more information you have before walking into the meeting, the better.

What's Next?

Next, let's take a look at some ways you can provide value to a connector and ask for more people to serve. First, we look at phrases to use with current clients. Then, we look at some phrases you can employ with nonclients.

CHAPTER 5

Give Value First

The first step in the G2G approach is to offer value to a referral-giver. As we mentioned in the last chapter, you must give to get.

Client- or Prospect-Generated Referrals

The G2G philosophy works well with clients. When you sell a product or service to a client and he or she is pleased with the results, you have the opportunity to ask for a referral. The key is to gauge how pleased your customer is with your offering. Only ask for a referral if you sense extreme satisfaction with your product or service offering.

You hear: Thanks so much for introducing me to your financial software package. It's meant a lot to our organization's bottom line.

You say: I sincerely appreciate that compliment. It means a lot to us when we're able to impact our clients' businesses like that. When we first met, you were struggling with cash flow, which was the challenge we really worked to address with our software. Can you think of another company like yours that's facing a similar problem that we might be able to help?

You hear: Yes. ABC, Ltd. could really use your services.

You say: Would you mind introducing me?

There's a narrow window when you'll be able to ask for referrals in this type of scenario. If you see the opportunity to ask for introductions from a very satisfied customer, jump at the chance. When you do, though, here's the formula: (1) show sincere gratitude for their comments, (2) remind the prospect why they hired you in the first place, and (3) ask whom they know who's facing a similar problem. Of course, you won't always know why they hired you. If that's the case, try this approach:

You hear: Your research report has made an incredible difference in the way our marketing team approaches their work. Thank you for the insight your firm provided.

You say: Thank you so much for that compliment. We really appreciate hearing from clients about what our research means to them. Do you mind telling me what caused you to decide to work with us in the first place?

You hear: Well, our marketing team was struggling with targeting our messages to our clients, and we needed a research firm to help us determine exactly what we should be saying to our target markets.

You say: That's interesting. Again, we are so glad to have made a difference for your organization. As you can imagine, the only way we can continue to provide this kind of work is by growing our client network. Do you know of anyone who's currently facing a similar challenge whom we might be able to reach out to?

The most important take-away from this strategy is to ask for a referral only after your customer or client has expressed significant fulfillment from your offering. To do otherwise is asking for referrals out of the blue. Show or tell them what you're giving to get that referral. It will not serve you well to ask for a referral before they have experienced your product or service.

Offering Other Value

On the other hand, you can earn referrals by determining what struggles or challenges a potential connector might be facing—even if those challenges are unrelated to what you sell!

You hear: Thanks for processing our latest order so quickly. We've been struggling with other vendors who aren't as responsive as you.

You say: You're welcome. We take our responsibilities seriously. Just curious, what vendors are you struggling with?

You hear: Our purple widget supplier has been slow to ship.

You say: May I introduce you to my friends over at Purple Widgets R Us? They're known for on-time delivery.

You hear: Absolutely, that would be great.

You say: I'll make that connection as soon as possible. While we're on the topic of referrals, do you know of anyone who might be looking for the kind of faster order processing I've been offering you?

This is G2G in a nutshell: earning the right to ask for referrals by giving value. Provide that value to a customer, even if it's outside your area of expertise, and you can feel confident in asking for referrals. Demonstrating your knowledge of areas beyond your product or service offering vastly improves your positioning and helps you earn a reputation of trusted partner.

Giving Great Service

The truth is that many of your prospects and customers will not openly confess their satisfaction with your product or service offering. The key in those cases is to ensure total satisfaction with your service. We mentioned earlier how critical it is to service an account beyond any reasonable level of expectation. High levels of service open an opportunity to ask for a referral.

You hear: You're really going above and beyond here. I appreciate your willingness to take my calls during the weekends. As you know, we have to keep everything running smoothly 24/7.

You say: It's my pleasure. I'm honored to be able to play a role on your organization's team. We believe it's essential that our clients receive nothing but the best service. In fact, I'd love to find more clients like you. Do you know of anyone who isn't getting serviced at the level they'd like?

You hear: Actually, my friend Maureen was recently complaining that her current supplier isn't willing to help her after 4:30 p.m.

Giving Concessions

During a negotiation, you might run into an opportunity to employ the G2G philosophy by offering concessions. This approach should be used sparingly because you risk cutting your price unnecessarily. Also, if you don't clearly understand what you're asking for in return, you risk never getting anything back.

You hear: You have to reduce the price. I can't pay anything over $45,000.

You say: If I give you a $5,000 discount, will you agree to arrange three meetings with qualified referrals?

Nonclient-Generated Referrals

What happens if there is no sales opportunity with someone who can introduce you to referrals? Can you still earn referrals? The answer is yes! Generating referrals from nonclients is simple, too. The key remains to follow the G2G philosophy. We go into a lot more detail about generating referrals from nonclients, but for now, let's take a look at a few suggestions for G2G in nonclient relationships.

Giving Great Recommendations (Even If They're Unrelated to What You Do)

Building goodwill, which is at the heart of the G2G philosophy, is accomplished by doing favors for others. One of the best ways to do that is to listen for opportunities to make great recommendations—even if they have nothing to do with your business.

You hear: I really could use a good painter. My husband and I are hoping to paint our house this summer.

You say: Chuck Radley is the best painter I've ever worked with. One of my other manufacturing clients hired Chuck to paint his house last year and has been raving about the results ever since.

You hear: We've been struggling with filling a customer service position. For some reason, we can't find any qualified applicants.

You say: Mind if I ask around? I know a number of people who are looking for that kind of role.

You hear: We're trying to figure out which soccer team my daughter should join.

You say: Hey, my friend Sam is the coordinator for the youth league. Would you like me to set up a meeting for you?

Looking for opportunities to help other people with challenges or questions they're facing often leads to favors being paid back to you.

Understand Their Referral Needs

By understanding what nonclient connectors look for when it comes to referrals, you can effectively employ the G2G strategy with them. Here's how that looks:

You say: Patrick, I know you work with optometrists and ophthalmologists. What would I need to know to give you referrals for your business?

You hear: Well, I'm looking for optometrists and ophthalmologists who are committed to leading-edge surgery for their patients. More specifically ABC.

You say: Okay. I've met a few optometrists and ophthalmologists in my work. Do you know Drs. X, Y, or Z?

You hear: No. Can you introduce me?

You say: Sure! I'll make these introductions in the next three days. How does that sound to you?

Now you've given. You've done your part. What you're hoping for now is that this person will "automatically" return the favor. And one of two things will happen. They will either immediately return the favor or they won't. We show you how to handle both situations.

Immediate Reciprocation

You hear: Wow! If you can make those introductions, that would be wonderful. Thank you for that. Is there anything I can do for you in return?

You say: Oh yes! As you know, I help hospital administrators design, develop, and install video monitors for laparoscopic surgeries. My ideal referrals are with hospital administrators and board members who are in the process of considering expanding, modernizing, or building new operating rooms. Whom do you know who might fit that description?

You hear: Have you met Gerry Malmo? He chairs the board of the Dodge County hospital, and it looks like they are going to receive a huge grant for expansion.

You say: No, I don't know him. How can we meet?

Because your nonclient connector offered you the opportunity to receive a favor of a referral in return, you were able to immediately provide your Direct Value Statement and describe the people you ideally work with. It's important to be clear at this point so your connector can more easily identify referrals for you. You may think that the broader you make your DVS, the more referrals you will receive, but the opposite is true. The more specific and focused you are, the more qualified referrals you'll receive.

Now, let's take a look at what happens if you offer a referral, but don't receive an offer of help in return.

No Immediate Reciprocation

You say: Patrick, I know you work with optometrists and ophthalmologists. What would I need to know to give you referrals for your business?

You hear: Well, I'm looking for optometrists and ophthalmologists who are committed to leading-edge surgery for their patients. More specifically ABC.

You say: Okay. I've met a few optometrists and ophthalmologists in my work. Do you know Drs. X, Y, or Z?

You hear: No. Can you introduce me?

You say: Sure! I'll make these introductions in the next three days. How does that sound to you?

You hear: Great! Thanks so much.

It's clear that, in this case, Patrick isn't immediately returning the favor of a referral. Here's what to do in such a case:

You say: How much do you know about what I do, Patrick?

You hear: Not much.

You say: Okay. I help hospital administrators design, develop, and install video monitors for laparoscopic surgeries. My ideal referrals are with hospital administrators and board members who are in the process of considering expanding, modernizing, or building new operating rooms. Whom do you know who might fit that description?

You hear: I really don't know anybody.

You say: Might some of the doctors you work with know any of the hospital administrators?

You hear: Yes. I could introduce you to Dr. Pickens. He knows everybody at Mass General.

You say: Thank you so much. When do you think we could all get together?

You didn't even ask for referrals, it just "automatically" happened. With the principle of G2G at work, it becomes second nature for people to help you.

Conclusion

The Give-to-Get philosophy is a great strategic approach to getting referrals. It's not about demanding them, expecting them, or even hoping for them. Instead, G2G is about providing value to others in accordance with the law of reciprocation: by doing things for other people, it's reasonable to expect them to return the favor.

If you do a good enough job of delivering value to connectors, they will eventually provide the river of referrals you're hoping to earn. In the following chapters we go into a lot more detail.

CHAPTER 6

Follow Through

Follow Through with Referrals

So many salespeople work hard to earn referrals and then never follow up with them. If you are honest with yourself and you carefully consider your past experiences, you will probably find that you also left opportunities on the table. In other words, if you have been in sales for a long time, you have probably been handed referral opportunities that you did not follow through on. If you repeatedly fall into this trap, go back and spend some more time reading Chapter 3.

Once you've earned the referral, follow through quickly. There are two scenarios for following up with referrals. A connector can either be active or passive. An active connector is willing to make introductions for you. A passive connector prefers that you reach out to a referral without his help. Here's how this works.

Active Connectors

You hear: Tom, I know your business is built on meeting commercial contractors. Have you met the people over at Landmark?

You say: No, but I've been trying to for years. Do you know them?

You hear: Yes. I know Jerry, the executive vice president, really well. I can make that introduction for you.

You say: What's the best way for us to connect? Would you rather contact Jerry first or should I go ahead and contact him?

You hear: I'll give him a call tomorrow.

This is an active connector. In other words, he's willing to make that introduction for you. This is almost always best.

You say: Okay, I'll give you a call in two days to see what our next step is.

Once an active connector has let you know that it's appropriate to contact the referral, here's what to say when you contact the referral:

You say: Tom Benson, a mutual friend of ours, asked me to give you a call, and I promised him I would.

Or, if an assistant answers the phone:

You say: Tom Benson, a mutual friend of Jerry [the referral] and mine, asked me to give him a call, and I promised I would.

Passive Connectors

On the other hand, you might have a passive connector.

You hear: Jillian, have you met Brooke Harris? She's looking for an architect, and I know you could really help her.

You say: That would be wonderful. What's the best way for us to meet? Would you rather contact Jillian first, or should I go ahead and reach out to her?

You hear: Why don't you just go ahead and let her know you and I spoke.

You say: Okay, great. I'll give her a call as soon as I'm able.

When you reach out:

You say: Philip Gose, a mutual friend of ours, asked me to give you a call, and I promised I would.

Or, if an assistant answers the phone:

You say: Philip Gose, a mutual friend of Brooke [the referral] and mine, asked me to give Brooke a call, and I promised I would.

Follow-Up with Connectors

Follow-through with a connector is as important as good follow-up with a referral. Once you have identified a good, qualified connector, maximize the relationship and show how grateful you are for it by following through properly. Here we highlight some powerful strategies.

Throughout the sales process with a referral, maintain contact with the connector who introduced you. This strategy ensures that you remain top-of-mind. Put another way, the more frequently a connector thinks of you, the more frequently you'll receive referral opportunities from that connector.

If you successfully follow up with your referral source, you will generate a constant river of referrals that means more opportunities in the future. Often, this isn't much more than sending a few e-mails.

Consistent Follow-Up

You write: Sherman, Rose and I are meeting next week. Again, thank you! I'll let you know how it goes. —Bill

Following the meeting, if it doesn't go well:

You write: Sherman, The meeting with Rose went well, although I can't help her. I suggested she contact Leslie. Again, thank you so much for the introduction! —Bill

If everything goes well:

You write: Sherman, The meeting with Rose went really well. Looks like we can truly help her. Thanks again. I'll keep you posted. —Bill

Continue to keep your connector up to date on what's happening in the relationship. In short, each time there's an agreed-upon meeting or action, update your connector. Thank him every time. This is an easy way to stand out from the crowd.

A Final Word of Thanks

Once the opportunity is closed (either won or lost), send a handwritten thank-you note to your connector.

You write:

Dear Sherman, Again, thank you for the opportunity to meet with Rose. By now, you know that she has entered into a contract with us. We look forward to providing her with our highest level of service. I rely on referrals and recommendations like the one you gave me with Rose. I can't tell you how grateful I am for the show of support you provided. Please don't hesitate to let me know how I can return the favor.

Sincerely,

Bill

Bill Robins

PART

PERFECT PHRASES FOR
REFERRALS FROM
NONCLIENTS

CHAPTER 7

Give Emotional Words

The emotional triggers outlined in this book are based on our original research. First developed for use exclusively in the political arena, we translated our methods and applied them to sales interactions. We observed more than 12,000 salespeople over a 20-year period. Our findings were then ready for real-world application to sales improvement and enhancement. Based on this research, we published the top-selling book *You're Working Too Hard to Make the Sale*.

Emotional words elicit an emotion in the listener's mind. For example, the word *chair* by itself doesn't elicit any emotion, but you can't hear the word *prestige* without having an emotional response to it. Prestige represents something that is powerfully expressive.

There are a handful of words that guarantee an emotional response. When you're talking with people and you use those words, you're speaking to their emotions, not only their logic. This is important because earning referrals is emotional. Speaking in emotional terms can move people to action. Here are a few words that guarantee an emotional response:

- Comfort
- Security
- Time
- Peace of mind
- Prestige

But that's only scratching the surface. In Chapter 8, we go into precise detail to show you which emotional words you can use with 38 types of prospects. And, we give you examples in four types of settings: face-to-face, on the phone, in e-mail, and with social media.

The Words That Sell

Since the first publication of our book *You're Working Too Hard to Make the Sale*, we have continued to develop the concept that certain words work with great precision in specific sales situations with varying customer types. As a result, we have produced an extensive library of terms and phrases that key decision makers respond to most favorably as they relate to the sales relationship, perception of products and services, benefits most sought, expectations of vendor delivery, and price. For example, the words that work best for a corporate CEO are not the same words that work best for an entrepreneurial leader.

We have taken the concepts and applied them to the highly critical referral request. They play a vital role in the G2G approach. As we discussed in the last chapter, you must provide meaningful value to a referral giver before asking for a referral.

Now, we outline the specific phrases that spur those referral-givers to respond favorably and readily with qualified referrals.

The Formula for Success

There's a simple formula to use. For nonclients, it looks like this:

It's important to me to work with my [occupation] clients in a way that [primary want]. [Our product/service] is [product and service want]. We are [provider want]. People hire us again and again because [benefit want] and [price want]. When I describe that, who comes to mind for you?

And, for clients, it looks like this:

As you've seen, I've tried to work with you in a way that [primary want]. [Our product/service] is [product and service Want]. We are [provider want]. People hire us again and again because [benefit want] and [price want]. When I describe that, who comes to mind for you?

Here's an example one of our clients used while speaking with a process engineer client:

As you've seen, I've tried to work with you in a way that lets you lead the project and call the shots. Our engineering software is cutting edge and innovative, just like your team's and organization's operations. We are dedicated to providing clients like you with process-oriented solutions and we relate to the engineering mentality. People hire us again and again because we understand process requirements and offer a competitive, justifiable rate. When I describe people we like to do business with and what we can offer them, who comes to mind for you?

For more examples, go to Chapter 8.

Needs versus Wants

Notice that in each formula, we're looking at customers' *wants*. For a long time, salespeople focused on customers' *needs*. The difference between the two centers on a unique concept: Prospects don't always buy what they need. They always, however, buy what they truly want.

Needs are:

- Product-specific: *I need a refrigerator.*
- Rational: *I need to stay within budget.*
- Above the surface: *I will freely share all of this information with you.*
- Based on fact: *I need the final product to be 5' × 10'.*

Wants, on the other hand, are:

- Product-neutral: *I want prestige in everything I buy.*
- Emotional: *I want to feel proud of what I buy.*
- Below the surface: *I won't tell you any of this information unless I trust you.*
- Based on perception: *I decide what feels prestigious.*

As a consequence, here's the principle:

For salespeople who can present their product or service (a need) in the way that their prospect wants to perceive it, a sale is far more likely.

Let's put it another way:

Prospects are more likely to buy what they need from salespeople who understand what the prospects really want.

Now, let's take a look at the meaning of each bracketed term in the formula. Again, here are the formulas:

For nonclients, it looks like this:

It's important to me to work with my [occupation] clients in a way that [primary want]. [Our product/service] is [product and service wants]. We are [provider want]. People hire us again and again because [benefit want] and [price want]. When I describe that, who comes to mind for you?

And, for clients, it looks like this:

As you've seen, I've tried to work with you in a way that [primary want]. [Our product/service] is [product and service want]. We are [provider want]. People hire us again and again because [benefit want] and [price want]. When I describe that, who comes to mind for you?

- **Primary Want:** The type of relationship that the prospect wants to have with a salesperson, supplier, or vendor. *For example, an entrepreneur wants to be in charge.*
- **Product or Service Wants:** The way the prospect wants to perceive the product or service he or she seeks. *For example, surgeons want products that are prestigious.*
- **Provider Want:** The type of ideal provider that a prospect wants to do business with in securing a product or service. *For example, accountants want providers who are financially stable.*
- **Benefit Want:** The perception of the benefits that a prospect wants to receive in any product or service. *For example, CEOs want benefits that resolve everyone's concerns.*
- **Price Want:** How the prospect wants to perceive the ideal price. *For example, engineers want prices that are stable.*

What does all of this mean? It means that when you're seeking referrals, you need to properly position, describe, and articulate in absolute terms each of these wants (primary, product/

service provider, benefit, and price) to the potential connectors before they will be able to readily identify referrals for you.

Specifically how you do this for each type of referral giver is described in the following pages. But first, let's talk more about how this works. For example, to an entrepreneur, the most important thing about any product or service is that it must be "practical, street smart, and designed for his unique situation." This trend holds, no matter what the product or service might be. Here's how you'd present your product or service, for example, to an entrepreneur:

> Before I get specific about our service and how it works, let me first say that it's street smart, practical, and will be designed for your unique situation. Now, let me describe it to you in detail ...

The purchasing manager wants to see any product or service as being "easy to understand, solid and safe, and not technically challenging." So, how would you present your product or service to this type of prospect? Here it is:

> Before I get specific about my product and how it works, let me first say that it's easy to understand, it's a solid and safe purchase, and it doesn't require a lot of technical education. Now, let me describe it to you in detail ...

Use this same technique to describe yourself, your product offering, and your company when you're seeking referrals.

Let's get started.

CHAPTER 8

Nonclient Phrases

N one of the statements in this section should ever stand on their own. To be most effective, you must provide value to a potential referral giver before you use these statements. For a recap on how to accomplish this, refer to Chapter 5.

This chapter explores nonclient phrases to use on the phone and in face-to-face conversations, via e-mail, and on social media platforms. Phrases for the phone and face-to-face are interchangeable. Phrases for e-mail are written to be shorter and to the point. E-mail is written so that in the event that it gets forwarded to the referral, it positions you well in his or her mind. Finally, the social media phrases are written to be concise and suitable for posting on a variety of social networking platforms.

Consider the following skills when you are seeking referrals by telephone. To be successful when selling on the phone, you must master the following six skills:

1. The discipline to stay on task
2. The concentration to stay focused
3. The ability to adhere to a systematic approach
4. Good verbal communication skills
5. A pleasant, engaging voice
6. The ability and resilience to handle refusal and rejection

When we refer to the job titles in the phrases, we encourage you to tailor them to the specific individuals you're looking to meet. For example, when we say, "With that introduction, can you think of any purchasing agents I should meet?" change that to "With that introduction, can you think of any purchasing agents at chemical companies I should meet?"

Let's get started looking at phrases for earning referrals from 38 types of connectors.

Principal Accountant

Accountants seek predictability that minimizes their personal vulnerability. Professional accountants face strict legal regulations with significant consequences for errors. Therefore, when you're seeking referrals to accountants, demonstrate your predictability and steadiness.

On the Phone

You say: When I'm working with accountants, it's important to me to work with them in a way that ensures predictability. [Our product/service] makes a manageable practice possible and makes doing business a pleasurable experience. We are financially stable and don't make extravagant claims. People hire us again and again because we value balance in all that we do, which means we bring balance back into their lives, too! On top of it, I always deliver a textbook price. When I describe that, who comes to mind for you?

Face-to-Face

You say: It's important to me when I'm working with accountants that we make sure they know how things are going to turn out. [Our product/service] compensates for what they haven't yet learned. We always take the time to go the extra mile so that we can offer a reasonable return on investment. People choose to work with me because I help put everything in proportion. Perhaps most important, I always price things according to a textbook formula. Knowing that, do you know anyone who would enjoy working with someone like me?

E-Mail

You write: I'm hoping you might know someone I can help. As you might know, I work with accountants in a way that's predictable and safe. I help them have a rewarding practice by being supportive and bringing balance into their lives. Do you know someone who fits that description? I'll follow up by phone in a few days.

Social Media

You post: Contact me if you know any accountants who want balance in their lives by developing a manageable practice.

Nonprincipal Architect

These architects want to have what we call "reflected" personal prestige. In other words, their prestige comes from the principal architect they work for. Nonprincipal architects also want to share in the creative experience in an environment where professional vulnerability is limited. Working as employees in someone else's firm gives these architects the opportunity to obtain the reflected personal prestige they seek.

When you're seeking referrals to nonprincipal architects, concentrate your focus on creativity and teamwork.

On the Phone

You say: I'm looking to work with architects who do work with unparalleled quality and are members of a first-rate team. I want to share [our product/service] with them because it provides significant value and is not overly technical. We are hired because we are sensitive to design priorities that enhance the professional environment, and our prices are fair, even to the most demanding observer. With that in mind, can you think of anyone who might want to work with someone like me?

Face-to-Face

You say: My ideal architect clients want to be as creative as possible without being reckless. [Our product/service] is user friendly and has an excellent reputation. And our company is able to see past a profit and loss statement because we're nonjudgmental and responsive. People hire us because we help them make a permanent statement at a price that's easily defensible. Do you know someone who might fit that description?

E-Mail

You write: It's been great working with you! I hope to find additional opportunities with architects. I like to work with prestigious architects on a first-rate team. Our responsive company provides a well-accepted, highly regarded [product/service]. Do you know anyone I might be able to reach out to? If so, let me know. Otherwise, I'll follow up with you in a day or two.

Social Media

You post: Seeking to provide prestigious architects with well-accepted, highly regarded [product/service]. Message me for more information.

Principal Architect

These decision makers want professional validation and acknowledgment of their value. They also want acceptance of their work as long as that acceptance isn't "compromised" by the client. Some architects consider themselves artists who have to work—for purely economic reasons—in an artistically illiterate and unappreciative world. From their perspectives, that means they constantly try to please people who lack true artistic judgment and taste.

When you're trying to get referrals to other architects, demonstrate your understanding of their creative and artistic sides.

On the Phone

You say: I like to work with architects in a way that ensures they're validated and that their creativity is the key to a successful project. [Our product/service] is unique, novel, and makes real creativity possible. We are sensitive to design priorities and are never judgmental. We work to enhance any environment we're a part of. Our prices are always easily defensible. So, with that in mind, what architects do you know who might fall into that category?

Face-to-Face

You say: I'm hoping to work with architects who use their own ideas to create projects that aren't compromised so they can make their own statements. [Our product/service] stands behind architects like that because it's practical, but not excessive. Our company is responsive and sympathetic to their needs. We want to help our clients make a permanent statement at a price that's fair, even to the most demanding observer. Knowing that, what architects come to mind?

E-Mail

You write: I'm hoping to partner with architects whose clients consider them creative artists. That's because [our product/service] makes real creativity possible since it's unique and innovative. We're sensitive to design priorities and nonjudgmental so that we can help them enhance the environments they build. Does that make you think of any architects I can meet? I'll give you a call in a few days to follow up on whom you have in mind.

Social Media

You post: Looking for architects to share my unique [product/service] to help them make real creativity possible. Message me if you know whom I can meet!

Litigating Attorney

A litigating attorney's need to control the environment and many aspects of the practice—particularly what happens in the courtroom—is directly attributable to the win-or-lose nature of this decision maker's work.

To say that his or her work environment is adversarial is to repeat an often-used word that really doesn't capture the essence of it. The word supposedly refers to the "adversarial" system of justice in which two attorneys, each representing his or her client, square off against each other. While that may be true, for a litigating attorney the contest isn't always simply the pursuit of justice or the rightful resolution of competing claims.

A substantial concern may be the defeat of their own personal adversary—the other attorney.

When you're seeking referrals to litigating attorneys, show your understanding of their desires for control and for a lack of emotional distractions.

On the Phone

You say: It's important to me to work with my attorney clients in a way that ensures they are in control and don't get emotionally bogged down so that they can keep on winning. [Our product/service] is sophisticated and well thought out. We are recognized for our credibility and tough mindedness. We get repeat business because of our bulletproof performance and adaptability. When I describe that kind of attorney, who comes to mind for you?

Face-to-Face

You say: It's important to me to work with my attorney clients in a way that helps them control the outcome—and do it without paying an emotional price. [Our product/service] is capable of quick implementation and gives attorney clients substantial competitive advantages. We are able to perform under difficult circumstances and we are often told we have our act together when times get tough. Attorneys hire us time and again because of our significant impact on them and because we are sensitive to their professional needs. With that description, who comes to mind for you?

E-Mail

You write: Do you know any litigating attorneys? Specifically, I'm looking for attorneys who don't get emotionally bogged down in their work, but keep on winning. [Our product/service] is well thought out and gives litigating attorneys a substantial competitive advantage. Our company's sound internal procedures allow us to perform under difficult circumstances. Our focus is helping our clients to significantly impact others at prices that are sensitive to what the professionals need. With that description in mind, can you think of someone who fits that description? If I don't hear back, I'll give you a call next week to talk about this some more.

Social Media

You post: Seeking referrals to litigating attorneys interested in substantial competitive advantages regardless of the circumstances. Message me with referrals.

Nonlitigating Attorney

Among the words that work are exposure, anticipate, and inoculate. Think of them as a tripod on which this decision maker's buying motivation stands. Put them together, and you have a revealing picture. The picture shows you an attorney who works in a way that keeps his or her "uniform clean."

For these attorneys, exposure means making an error that could come back to haunt them in the form of litigation. They're not litigators. They don't have the desire or the temperament for it. As one particularly successful real estate attorney once told us, "Those guys who litigate are the paratroopers. I could never do what they do."

But they know that sooner or later some contract they write or some deal they approve is going to wind up in court. The odds are too great for it to be otherwise. And their worst fear is making that fatal mistake.

When you're looking for referrals to nonlitigating attorneys, be sure to highlight your understanding of these factors.

On the Phone

You say: When I'm working with attorneys, I prefer to work with them in a way that allows them to minimize their exposure and avoid major mistakes. It's easy because [our product/ service] is completely predictable and nearly automatic. Our company runs like a clock and leaves nothing to chance. We do everything to reduce our clients' dependence on other people at a price that takes professional priorities into account. With that in mind, can you think of someone whom I might be able to meet with?

Face-to-Face

You say: I'm hoping you might be able to provide me with some referrals to attorneys. Specifically, I'm looking for attorneys who do everything they can to make sure things stay out of court and are good at anticipating future events. [Our product/service] makes things happen for them as automatically as possible to ensure precise and predictable performance. We spell everything out and leave nothing to chance. I'm looking for attorneys who want to be free of people dependence and I can do so at a price that's sensitive to what the professional needs. Can you think of someone whom I may be able to help?

E-Mail

You write: I work best with attorneys who want to inoculate themselves—and their clients—against risk. [My product/ service] is precise in that it's completely predictable. Our zero failure rate makes sure no one throws a wrench into my clients' futures. Can you think of someone I might be able to help? I'll follow up with you in a day or two.

Social Media

You post: Looking to meet attorneys interested in a predictable source for [product/service]. Know anyone? Message me!

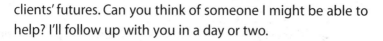

Nonentrepreneurial CEO with an Engineering Background

Most of these decision makers want to have guaranteed career survival in an environment where personal accountability is minimal and risk is shared. While the nonentrepreneurial CEO with a finance background is deeply concerned about financial stability, this type with the engineering background is more concerned with quantification.

When starting out as an engineer, he or she wanted to be in a profession where the crucial decisions didn't require speculation, intuition, or anything less than self-evident quantification.

The idea of quantification implies that decisions don't have to be entrusted to error-prone human judgment. Whenever factors go into that decision, they can be measured—quantified— with an impersonal, objective set of numbers, formulas, or algorithms. Thus, the ideal business is one in which the crucial decisions are reduced to mathematical calculations whose validity is beyond question.

When you're looking for referrals to this type of decision maker, highlight your understanding of the need to minimize risk and predictability.

On the Phone

You say: When I'm working with my CEO clients, I prefer to help them minimize risks to protect what they've built by establishing fail-safe predictability in all we do together. [Our product/service] protects them from the human factor and is proven reliable. We have a large installed base and our designs come from real-world applications. That leads to no surprises, no guesswork, and a stable price that's not subject to wide swings. Can you think of someone whom I might be able to serve in that way?

Face-to-Face

You say: I'm hoping to meet CEOs who want to make sure that important decisions are quantified and that every decision is beyond question. I'd like to help them with [our product/service] because it's an industry standard with tested reliability. Our proven designs are used throughout [industry], and we work hard to stabilize the work environment with controllable progress. Finally, I always make sure there are no radical shifts in our price. With that said, can you think of any CEOs who might be interested in meeting with me?

E-Mail

You write: I like to help CEOs make their businesses run predictably by using our tested [product/service]. Our company has a large installed base that enjoys no surprises, thanks to our overall stability. Do you know any CEOs I could meet? I'll give you a call in a few days to talk about whom you have in mind.

Social Media

You post: Can you introduce me to any CEOs looking to minimize the "human factor" as it relates to their [product/service] benefit? If so, let me know!

Nonentrepreneurial CEO with a Financial Background

Most of these decision makers want to have guaranteed career survival in an environment where risk is shared among the team and decisions are made on a factual, scientific basis.

Before they became CEOs, these decision makers had a particular view of the other senior managers in their companies. The other divisional and departmental managers—marketing, engineering, sales, production, and so on—had greater tolerance for risk than this decision maker did.

These executives consider tolerance a weakness because it could, in their opinion, put the companies in dangerous positions. Unlike most entrepreneurs, for example, these decision makers can easily perceive the down side associated with risk, while placing less importance on the up side.

When you're looking to earn referrals to this type of decision maker, highlight your ability to minimize risk.

On the Phone

You say: I prefer to work with CEOs in a way that minimizes their risks by moving forward one step at a time with an eye to advancing their career. [Our product/service] is free of controversy and interruptions. We operate in a stable, widely accepted, restrained way. People typically choose to do business with us because we put the right standards in place to make sure our clients and their companies don't lose their moorings. We do it all at a prudent price. With that introduction, do you know of anyone who might like to work with a person like me?

Face-to-Face

You say: I'm hoping you can connect me with CEOs who are looking to make major career investments that will insulate them and spread the risk by going straight down the middle. Those are the kinds of people I'd like to meet because [our product/service] stays on an even keel and keeps everything controllable by taking the key standards into account. Our company is financially stable, never makes extravagant claims, and our people don't get carried away. We create a solid foundation with our clients at a price that's thought through. Can you think of someone whom I might be able to connect with?

E-Mail

You write: My ideal clients are CEOs who believe there's no substitute for operating by the numbers. They hire me because I'm sensible and no-nonsense, and everything I do is designed with finances and operations in mind to keep people off their backs. Do you know anyone like that whom I might be able to serve? If so, let me know. I'll give you a call tomorrow.

Social Media

You post: Do you know any no-nonsense CEOs who believe knowing is better than guessing? If so, let me know because I can help them. Message me!

General Nonentrepreneurial CEO

There's a simple way to capture the essence of what this decision maker wants: Instead of playing to win, he plays not to lose. The nonentrepreneurial CEO's overriding goal is to survive professionally with a decent amount of respectability while he continues to move gradually and patiently up the corporate ladder.

This is a nonentrepreneurial professional who's content to have her career move along a conservatively plotted course. She takes only one cautious step at a time in a long series of such careful milestones.

These decision makers are driven, therefore, by an urgent desire for self-protection. Such a need can override the traits we typically associate with the character of the American businessperson: ambitious, goal oriented, competitive, etc. For that reason, it's more difficult to excite a nonentrepreneurial CEO about a product or service by claiming that it will produce brilliant results.

Instead, when you're trying to earn referrals from this type of decision maker, highlight your ability to help him operate cautiously and respectably.

On the Phone

You say: I prefer to work with CEOs who go straight down the middle to protect what they've built. That works well because [our product/service] is free of controversy and integrates without disrupting anything. We are respectable, restrained, and moderate. We have that reputation because we work hard to get everyone's agreement while making sure we resolve everyone's concerns. We do it all at a prudent price. With that kind of description, can you think of someone I might be able to help?

Face-to-Face

You say: Can you introduce me to any CEOs? Specifically, I'd prefer to work with people who look to spread the risk and who seek solutions that won't produce any arguments, because that's what [our product/service] does. We keep everything controllable and don't cause any interruptions. People hire us again and again because we don't believe in rocking the boat. We work hard to put everyone's possible objections to rest and achieve consensus. We do it all at a well-thought-through price. Who comes to mind?

E-Mail

You write: I need to meet some career-minded CEOs who are looking to protect what they've built by adopting [our product/service], because it won't produce any arguments from others. That's the case because we know how things are supposed to be done and don't make any demands on our clients. Instead, we make them look good by getting everyone on board early. Do you know anyone who might be looking for [our product/service] from a supplier like me? If so, let me know. Otherwise, I'll follow up in a day or two.

Social Media

You post: Contact me if you know any CEOs looking for [our product/service] who might benefit from meeting me. We're on an even keel and don't rock the boat.

Nonentrepreneurial CEO with an Operations Background

As enthusiastic as some decision makers are about abstract theories and models, nonentrepreneurial CEOs with operations backgrounds are just as wed to concrete reality. They deeply mistrust anything that seems complicated or abstract, being more comfortable with what's perceived as the real world.

They're hands-on people with no intellectual pretensions. In fact, most of them believe they have to "produce" in much the same way an auto mechanic believes he will never survive many bad repair jobs. Meanwhile, that mechanic is thoroughly convinced that the service manager can get by on the strength of her interpersonal skills or whatever other intangible virtue the service manager supposedly has that the mechanic doesn't.

Just like the relationship between the mechanic and the service manager, this type of executive believes that, unlike the fate of many others in the corporate community, her personal fortunes rest squarely on performance. It's not just performance in some abstract or intellectual sense, but a very physical sort of performance. These decision makers can only relate comfortably to what they perceive as being concrete and tangible. It's almost as if they believe "if you can't touch it, it doesn't exist."

When you're seeking referrals to decision makers like these, focus on your understanding of their desires for organization and their clear-cut environments.

On the Phone

You say: I'm hoping to meet CEOs who have created clear-cut environments in which everything is organized so their companies are humming along. [Our product/service] has built-in simplicity so that it's easy for people to use. We are just regular, down-to-earth people who want to help our clients maintain the performance they want. We do it at a price that's always stable. Given that context, do you know of any CEOs like that whom I should meet?

Face-to-Face

You say: I prefer to work with my CEO clients in a way that helps them get things organized and keeps everything buttoned down. That works well because [our product/service] is easy to figure out. Our company is made of regular people who understand that our clients' ideas and opinions matter. We believe in generating consistent outcomes so you can keep getting the results our clients want. We do all of this at a price that's not subject to wide swings. Do you know of any CEOs who might be looking for a partner like that?

E-Mail

You write: The CEOs I work best with are those who have everything in place in clear-cut environments. They like [our product/service] because it's not rocket science. It's really easy for people to use. We're just regular people who think the way our clients do. We're straightforward and believe in producing consistent results. It's easy for our clients to get their arms around what they want and hold onto it. Do you know any CEOs like that whom I might be able to meet? I'll give you a call tomorrow to talk about whom you have in mind.

Social Media

You post: Seeking to meet highly organized, operationally minded CEOs looking for a down-to-earth [product/service] supplier. Message me with suggestions!

Chief Financial Officer

Imagine a scale from +10 to –10 where 0 represents the absence of risk, +10 is the most risky situation, and –10 is the greatest possible distance one can move away from risk. For most technical decision makers, design engineers for example, anything from 0 to –10 is acceptable. Of course, they'd like to be exclusively in the minus column but they can tolerate "pure zero," particularly if they're in cutting-edge applications.

Most entrepreneurs are willing to live and work on the plus end of the spectrum. For the chief financial officer (CFO), pure zero isn't sufficient. Nor is he comfortable at the higher end of the minus side (e.g., –1, –2, –3, etc.). This decision maker can make the design engineer look like a wild gambler by comparison.

The same comparison can be made between the CFO and the other senior managers in the company. The other divisional managers—sales, marketing, engineering, production, and so on—have greater tolerance for risks than the CFO. That tolerance is considered a weakness by typical CFOs because it could, in their opinions, put the companies into dangerous positions.

As a result, most CFOs consider themselves the companies' "last lines of defense." They protect the companies from the weaknesses of others in the senior ranks.

When you're looking for referrals to CFOs, it's essential to address that need for risk mitigation.

On the Phone

You say: I'd like to meet CFOs who want to move risk as far away from themselves as possible and keep a big margin between themselves and dangerous risks. Those are the kinds of people I like to work with because [our product/

service] is balanced, designed with finances and operations in mind, and keeps people out of your hair. We're a sensible, no-nonsense company that doesn't make extravagant claims. We have everything running like clockwork so people aren't knocking on your door. And we do it all at a textbook price. With that in mind, what CFOs come to mind whom I might be able to serve?

Face-to-Face

You say: There is no substitute for operating by the numbers. At least that's my philosophy and the way I prefer to work with my CFO clients. [Our product/service] doesn't make them depend on guesswork and takes their key standards into account. Our company has a financial impact that is proportionate to the price and gives you a reasonable return on investment. We are able to keep things on track so that our clients can maintain control over what's really important. We do all of this at a price that's determined by a textbook formula. With that explanation, do you know any CFOs whom I might meet?

E-Mail

You write: I like to work with CFOs who believe knowing is always better than guessing. That's because [our product/service] is based on what a business is all about—the numbers. Our company is made up of people who don't get carried away, so they can give our clients reasonable returns on their investments. People hire us because when we get involved, they can maintain control over what is really important. With that description, who comes to mind? I'll follow up in a few days to discuss whom you think would benefit from working with me.

Social Media

You post: Looking to meet CFOs who believe there's no substitute for operating by the numbers. Let me know who comes to mind!

Chief Information Officer

Most chief information officers (CIOs) have expansive attitudes toward their own power/influence bases, primarily because they perceive those bases to be too limited and potentially jeopardized by user departments. It's a limitation that is firmly grounded in the history of the CIO's application and the traditional relationship between management information systems (MIS) people and the other people in their companies.

Gaining a certain mastery over relationships is a goal of the CIO, and the chief instruments for gaining that mastery are influence and authority. CIOs can't just "go along" without expressing at least some resistance. They often raise concerns about any number of conditions that conflict with their personal interests, and they have no patience for anything that compromises their authority and influence.

When you're attempting to earn referrals to CIOs, it's important to focus on your ability to help them maintain control and earn influence.

On the Phone

You say: When I'm working with my CIO clients, I like to help them maintain control and be influential in their roles. I can do that because [our product/service] is state of the art and has useful, practical value. Aside from that, it's an excellent tool for gaining and keeping authority. Our company is technically innovative. We're also told that we are a good alliance partner because we help our CIO clients gain more leverage to keep advancing toward their goals. We do it all at a price that can easily be defended. Does that make you think of anyone I might be able to meet?

Face-to-Face

You say: I'm looking to meet CIOs who aren't stopped from getting what they want. [Our product/service] is truly innovative with real-world value. It's certainly not run of the mill. Our company is constantly pushing the envelope. We help our clients gain ground by having control and being able to use it whenever, wherever, and however they want. And no one will get stuck with a price that makes people wonder. With that in mind, do you know of any CIOs I can meet?

E-Mail

You write: Do you know any CIOs? Specifically, I'm looking to meet those who aren't stopped from getting what they want inside their organizations. I work well with them because [our product/service] is novel, prestigious, and cutting edge. We are a technically innovative company that helps our clients keep gaining ground. Do you know of anyone I might be able to meet? If so, let's talk about it next week. I'll give you a call on Monday.

Social Media

You post: Looking to meet CIOs who understand you have to move ahead to stay ahead. Any introductions? Message me!

Chiropractor

Most chiropractors want to have professional respectability equivalent to that of physicians. Furthermore, they want their services to be perceived as scientific, necessary, and therapeutically legitimate. However, many chiropractors face challenges with their own patients. As one put it: "Chiropractors sometimes wind up with the treatment of junkies and neurotics who keep bouncing from one panacea to another."

When you're attempting to gain referrals to chiropractors, you need to emphasize your understanding of the unique nature of this decision maker's area of expertise.

On the Phone

You say: I'm hoping to meet chiropractors who recognize that no professional offers more unique or valuable services than they do. We recognize how important it is that [our product/service] helps our clients remain at the leading edge of healthcare. [Our product/service] has stood the test of time and is completely proven. Our company is open minded and ready to join forces with our chiropractor clients. We are hired over and over, largely because we help our clients get the results other treatments don't obtain. All of it comes at a price that gives them great returns on investments. With that in mind, can you think of any chiropractors I can meet?

Face-to-Face

You say: Are you able to introduce me to any chiropractors? Specifically, I'm looking for those who provide vital, mainstream, scientifically valid care. [Our product/service] serves them well because it has stood the test of time and is popular with the mainstream. Its well-known track record makes it a proven winner. We're selected by many chiropractors because we are ready to join forces with them and be unique right along with them. We make good partners in what always becomes healthy partnerships. My clients' patients can count on them, so there's no need to justify their services. And [our product/service] comes at a price that adds to our clients' potential for return on investment. With that in mind, can you think of someone I might be able to serve?

E-Mail

You write: I'm looking to meet chiropractors who are at the leading edge of healthcare and are looking for a [product/service] provider that has stood the test of time. Our company is willing to do what it takes to break new ground because we're not hung up on our own way of doing things. Let me know who comes to mind. I'll follow up in a day or two.

Social Media

You post: Looking for introductions to leading chiropractors who are looking for a cutting-edge provider of [product/service]. Message me with suggestions. Thanks!

Corporate Executive

The typical corporate executive (non-CEO) wants to be a well-thought-of team player who is comfortably anonymous and never singled out for extraordinary responsibilities. At the same time, he or she doesn't want to be left out of important processes and decisions.

For corporate executives, the notion of teamwork and being a team player is vital. These executives have an inordinate need for collective participation because within the confines of the group is a comforting and protective anonymity, not from others within the company, but from the outside world.

Be sure to discuss steady advancement, involvement, and teamwork when you're trying to get referrals to corporate executives.

On the Phone

You say: I'm hoping to meet [job title(s)] who are advancing steadily, are involved in all the important decisions, and work to keep everything on a safe course. These kinds of people benefit from [our product/service] because it's not a departure from what they're doing. Our company is widely accepted because it is made up of good team players. We are hired because we provide outcomes that everyone accepts. We always offer prices that are in the mainstream. With that kind of description, what [job title(s)] come to mind whom I might be able to serve?

Face-to-Face

You say: I'd like to be introduced to [job title(s)] who keep everything on a safe course by staying in the mainstream.

That's because [our product/service] supports what they have already accomplished. We blend in well with everyone because we're committed to a team approach. People choose to work with us because we generate the results that everyone accepts. We do it all at a price that's in line with the industry. With that in mind, can you think of someone I could help?

E-Mail

You write: I'm looking to be introduced to [job title(s)] who keep advancing steadily because [our product/service] is not a departure from what they are already doing. We are a widely accepted provider of [product/service]. Please let me know who comes to mind. I'll follow up by phone in a few days.

Social Media

You post: Looking to help [job title(s)] who are keeping everything on a safe course because [our product/service] supports what they've already accomplished.

Entrepreneurial Dentist/Orthodontist

In the medical profession, dentists are often perceived as more prestigious than chiropractors, but less so than surgeons. However, no amount of prestige would be a source of much comfort to dentists if they didn't also have a significant amount of orderliness in their lives. This decision maker has to make an investment that most other healthcare providers can avoid.

Neurosurgeons make relatively modest investments in the tools of their trade to go into practice. Radiologists work with someone else's imaging equipment until the more entrepre-

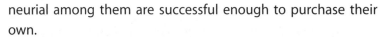

neurial among them are successful enough to purchase their own.

However, dentists are faced with two choices: First, they can work in someone else's practice, or second, they can put themselves at potential financial risk for the privilege of being entrepreneurial.

Because these dentists choose to be entrepreneurs, they need to perceive that their futures will unfold according to the ideal formula. They want their professional lives to follow the paths they learned about when they studied successful independent dental practices in dental school.

When you're seeking referrals to dentists or orthodontists who have chosen the entrepreneurial path, be sure to show them that working with you is not a gamble.

On the Phone

You say: Can you introduce me to any dentists or orthodontists? Specifically, I'd like to meet those who believe everything should happen the way they plan it. That's because our uncomplicated [product/service] doesn't require much attention. Our company believes there's no substitute for honesty and hides nothing. To protect their professional privacy, we guard our clients from situations they don't want. And we do it all at a price that's directly related to value. Who comes to mind?

Face-to-Face

You say: When I work with dentists and orthodontists, I prefer to work with them in a way that's orderly and provides no unpleasant surprises. After all, I don't want to distract my clients from practicing their art. [Our product/service] is practical and uncomplicated. Our company offers simple, straightforward answers, and we keep challenges and obstacles at a distance. When it comes to our prices, it's easy to translate the costs into value.

E-Mail

You write: I'm hoping you can introduce me to dentists/orthodontists who don't like anything that distracts them from practicing their art. Our plain-talk company offers simple, straightforward answers and protects our clients from situations they don't want. Can you think of any dentists/orthodontists I could meet? If so, let me know. I'll give you a call in a few days.

Social Media

You post: Can you introduce me to any dentists/orthodontists looking for more time to practice their art? I can help them. Please message me!

Design Engineer

This decision maker wanted to be in a profession where the important decisions wouldn't require speculation, intuition, or anything less than self-evident quantification. The idea of quantification implies that decisions don't have to be entrusted to flawed human judgment. Whatever factors go into that decision can be measured—quantified—with an impersonal and objective set of numbers, or formulae, or algorithms.

Thus, the design engineer's ideal work environment is one in which the crucial decisions are reduced to mathematical calculations whose validity is beyond question. This is the world in which most design engineers wanted to work when they set out on their careers and the reason they have such an obsession for collecting data and supporting information before they make a decision.

When you're attempting to earn referrals to design engineers, highlight a fail-safe, systematic approach.

On the Phone

You say: When working with my design engineer clients, we help them establish fail-safe predictability so they are able to quantify everything. [Our product/service] protects them from the "human factor" because it's reliable, tested, and proven. People hire our company time and again because of our large installed base and our quantified designs. Proven designs are collected and incorporated into [our product/service]. It stabilizes the work environment, all at a price that's not subject to wide swings. Do you know any design engineers who like to work that way?

Face-to-Face

You say: Can you introduce me to any design engineers who make sure that their important decisions are quantified? That is the kind of design engineer I'd like to work with because [our product/service] is a proven industry standard. Our company collects proven designs from real-world applications and uses them in our large installed base. We don't rely on guesswork and we avoid surprises. That helps us work with clients at a price that's not subject to wide swings. Can you think of someone whom I could meet?

E-mail

You write: Can you introduce me to any design engineers? Specifically, I'm looking to meet those who make sure their important decisions are quantified, because [our product/service] minimizes the "human factor." Our quantified designs eliminate guesswork. With that explanation, can you think of any design engineers I can meet? I'll give you a call in the next day or two to discuss whom you have in mind.

Social Media

You post: Looking to meet design engineers who are interested in minimizing the "human factor" and eliminating guesswork. Message me with names!

Entrepreneur with an Engineering Background

Like most other types of entrepreneurs, this one wants to be personally independent. He or she wants to be free from the control, domination, or influence of any kind of boss. However, where the entrepreneur with a financial background has a desire for a financially stable business, this type is more concerned with quantification.

When starting out on a career as an engineer, he or she wanted to be in a profession where the crucial decisions didn't require speculation, intuition, or anything less than self-evident quantification. The ideal business would be one in which the crucial decisions are reduced to mathematical calculations whose validity is beyond question. This is the world in which the engineer wanted to work when he or she set out on a career.

When you're looking for referrals to entrepreneurs with engineering backgrounds, emphasize independence and stability.

On the Phone

You say: I prefer to work with clients who like being in charge and calling their own shots, because [our product/service] is

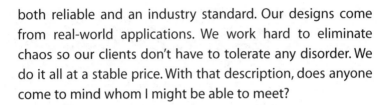

both reliable and an industry standard. Our designs come from real-world applications. We work hard to eliminate chaos so our clients don't have to tolerate any disorder. We do it all at a stable price. With that description, does anyone come to mind whom I might be able to meet?

Face-to-Face

You say: My clients tell me they enjoy working with me because I help them make their businesses run their way. I work hard to help them make their businesses run with fail-safe predictability. I say that because our [product/service] has been tested and proven in terms of its reliability. We have a large installed base that provides our clients with order in their businesses. And we do it all at a price that's not subject to wide swings. Can you think of anyone whom you might be able to introduce me to?

E-Mail

You write: I'm looking to meet business owners who have complete control over their businesses. [Our product/service] helps them, because it minimizes the "human factor" and allows my clients to exercise their personal independence. We use proven designs throughout our large installed base and bring order to every business we work with. Knowing that about my clients, who comes to mind? I'll give you a call tomorrow so we can discuss this further.

Social Media

You post: Hoping to help business owners who want to make their businesses run predictably with our proven [product/service]. Message me for more information.

Entrepreneur with a Financial Background

Like most other types of entrepreneurs, this one wants to be personally independent. He or she wants to be free from the control, domination, or influence of any kind of boss. However, there's also a big desire here for a level of financial stability, which the other entrepreneur types don't feel as urgently.

Most entrepreneurs, including this type, aren't trying to build financial empires for themselves. For the most part, they went into business because they wanted to achieve a far more limited goal of a respectable income without having to put up with a boss. And in the case of this type of entrepreneur, that income must be guaranteed by a financially stable business.

Having enough cash to pay themselves, their employees, and their creditors is the foremost priority. The concept of financial stability, however, is an abstraction for other entrepreneurs. Typically, only entrepreneurs with financial backgrounds can truly grasp and "feel" the significance of financial stability.

When you're looking for referrals to this type of buyer, highlight this financial stability and independence.

On the Phone

You say: My ideal client is a business owner with a financially stable business run by the numbers. That's because [our product/service] is designed with finances and operations in mind. We don't make extravagant claims because our work has a financial impact that's proportionate to the price. We provide order that reflects our clients' wishes to keep their internal systems and procedures running smoothly. And we do it all at a textbook price. With that kind of explanation, who comes to mind?

Face-to-Face

You say: I prefer working with clients who make their businesses run the way they want them to so they have guaranteed futures. We work well together because [our product/service] takes the key priorities into account and doesn't make them dependent on guesswork. We are a sensible, financially stable company. We never tolerate disorder and we run quantifiably. We price everything according to a textbook formula. Given that description, who comes to mind?

E-Mail

You write: I help business owners call their own shots and make their businesses run their way. That's because [our product/service] is based on what a business is all about: the numbers. We are a sensible, no-nonsense organization that helps our clients avoid chaos. Can you think of someone who might be looking for a provider like me? I'll follow up by phone in a day or two so we can discuss anyone you have in mind.

Social Media

You post: We help our clients make their businesses run by the numbers because [our product/service] is designed with finances and operations in mind. Can you think of someone who would benefit?

Entrepreneur

Most entrepreneurs aren't trying to build financial empires for themselves. Most of them went into business to achieve a far more limited goal: a steady, respectable paycheck without having to put up with a boss. These decision makers could never accept a position in a large organization, no matter how prestigious or well paying it might be.

Entrepreneurs tend to clash with authority that's exerted over them. As a result, the desire for personal independence drives entrepreneurs to start their own businesses. The impulse isn't only profit or riches. It's freedom.

That's an important distinction because it tells you the best way to seek referrals to this type of decision maker and the approaches you should avoid.

When you're looking to earn referrals to entrepreneurs, it's more important to emphasize freedom and independence than profit and money.

On the Phone

You say: I'm hoping you can introduce me to some people who call their own shots and have complete control over their businesses. That's because there is nothing theoretical or abstract about [our product/service]. Instead, it's designed for [the specific kind of business you're hoping to be referred to]. We are accommodating because we recognize each of our clients' unique situations, and we eliminate the chaos that many business owners complain about. Can you think of someone who might be interested in meeting me?

Face-to-Face

You say: My clients tell me they work with me because I help them have complete control over their businesses. Our completely customized solutions are practical and designed for specific client situations. Our organization is flexible, responsive, and willing to do whatever it takes to make sure every detail is covered. That's because we work hard to provide the order and control our clients expect. Can you think of any business owners who might like to work with a provider like me?

E-Mail

You write: I'm hoping to meet some business owners who make their businesses run their way. That's because [our product/service] is designed specifically for their unique situations [e.g., for small businesses]. We work hard to make sure every detail is covered so that we reflect our clients' personal wishes. Can you think of someone whom you might be able to introduce me to? I'll follow up by phone in a few days.

Social Media

You post: Looking to meet business owners with complete control over their businesses, because [our product/service] is designed specifically for them. Message me with suggestions!

Entrepreneur with an Operations Background

Like most other types of entrepreneurs, this one wants to be personally independent. He or she wants to be free from the control, domination, or influence of any kind of boss.

As enthusiastic as some decision-maker types are about abstract theories and models, entrepreneurs with operations backgrounds are just as wed to concrete reality. They deeply mistrust anything that seems complicated or abstract, being more comfortable with what's perceived as real world and hands-on.

These entrepreneurs have a virtual passion for keeping everything humming along. Orderliness and routine are of paramount importance to these entrepreneurs because nothing will "hum" in the presence of disorganization. Everything must be in its place in their worlds, just as things were when they worked for someone else.

Emphasizing your ability to create and maintain orderliness is essential when seeking referrals to this kind of decision maker.

On the Phone

You say: Can you help me meet any entrepreneurs? Specifically, I'm looking to meet people who call their own shots in a clear-cut environment where everything is in its place. [Our product/service] is designed specifically for their unique situations [e.g., for small businesses]. We are regular, down-to-earth people who help maintain the performance our clients want. We do it all at a price that's stable. With that overview, can you think of anyone you can introduce me to?

Face-to-Face

You say: When I work with my clients, I prefer to work with them in a way that allows them to call their own shots so they can have everything in its place. [Our product/service] is designed specifically for their unique situations [e.g., for small businesses] and won't put any demands on their time or strain their resources. We are straightforward and we believe our clients' opinions and ideas matter. Our clients work with us over and over again because we keep getting the results they want. And we do it all at a stable price. Can you think of someone whom I might be able to serve?

E-Mail

You write: I'm hoping you can introduce me to some entrepreneurs you might know who have everything in place and keep things organized and orderly. Those are the kinds of people we're able to help because [our product/service] is designed specifically for people who run their businesses like that. [Our product/service] is practical and won't strain their resources. When we work with clients, we're down-to-earth and work hard to get the consistent results they want. Who comes to mind? I'll follow up by phone in a few days to talk about this more.

Social Media

You post: We help entrepreneurs make the businesses run their way … by keeping everything in place. Whom can we help?

Equipment Engineer

In any environment where equipment plays a crucial part, most equipment engineers actually play roles that are inconsistent with their importance.

For people with such heavy responsibilities, equipment engineers don't enjoy as much respect as others in that environment, particularly those who are members of the purchasing committee or other types of engineers. In a typical manufacturing environment, for example, the process engineer and the design engineer are thought of as the elite members of the team. Meanwhile, the equipment engineers don't have the same amount of decision-making authority, influence, or prestige.

Although they're certainly proud of the work they do, most equipment engineers are deeply annoyed and offended by the prejudices held against them.

As a result, when you're trying to build referrals to equipment engineers, focus on your understanding that they are deserving of as much authority as the others.

On the Phone

You say: I'm hoping to meet more equipment engineers whom I can serve. I believe no one does more crucial work than they do because nothing can happen without them. [Our product/service] has built-in simplicity and is easy to figure out. But it's also rugged and durable. Engineers choose to work with me because I respond quickly and we can turn on a dime. That helps my clients be included sooner in important decisions. And we do it all at a stable price. With that description, can you think of someone whom I might be able to serve?

Face-to-Face

You say: My business is built on equipment engineers so I would like to meet more. I recognize that their work is as important as anyone else's and they deserve as much authority as anyone else. [Our product/service] is easy for people to use and can take a lot of punishment. We provide our clients with an instant response when they need us, which helps them get their rightful places in making decisions. And we do it all at a stable price. Does anyone come to mind who might be interested in working with someone like me?

E-Mail

You write: I like to work with engineers who know that nothing can happen without them. [Our product/service] can stand up under a lot of wear and tear. As a company, we are known for our quick response to our clients and the value we place on their input. Can you think of anyone who might enjoy working with someone like me? If so, let me know. I'll give you a call next week.

Social Media

You post: No one does more crucial work than equipment engineers. That's why I'm hoping to help them with our ruggedly reliable [product/service]. Message me if you know anyone!

Facilities Manager

As enthusiastic as some decision makers are about abstract theories and models, facilities managers are just as wed to concrete reality. They are wary of anything that seems complicated or abstract, being more comfortable with what's perceived as real world and hands on. As you might expect, they have no desire to deal in ambiguities.

These decision makers can only relate comfortably to what they perceive as being concrete and tangible. It's almost as if they believe "if you can't touch it, it doesn't exist."

To earn referrals to facilities managers, be sure to emphasize the clear-cut, real-world, and hands-on nature of what you do.

On the Phone

You say: When I work with facilities managers, I prefer to work with them in a way that's clear cut, real world, and hands on. That's exactly how [our product/service] works with its built-in simplicity. Our team is made up of down-to-earth people who think the way our clients do. We are hired because we maintain the performance our clients want, which leads to consistent results. And we do it all at prices that aren't subject to wide swings. With that overview, can you think of any facilities managers you can introduce me to?

Face-to-Face

You say: It's important to me to work with my facilities manager clients in a way that emphasizes the real-world performance they expect. That fits nicely because [our product/service] is not rocket science and is easy for people to use. Our company is made up of people who are straightforward, whose mission is to help our clients get the consistent results they want. And we do it at a price without any radical shifts. What facilities managers come to mind?

E-Mail

You write: Facilities managers work with me because I provide them with tangible, real-world explanations. They also like [our product/service] because of its built-in simplicity. We're regular people who work hard and think like our clients. We are called on time and again because we keep getting the results our clients want. We help them get their hands on what they want and hold onto it. Can you think of anyone who might like to meet with someone like me? If so, let's have a conversation about this. I'll give you a call tomorrow.

Social Media

You post: Looking to help more facilities managers with concrete, clear-cut solutions to [the problems your product/service solve]. Message me with suggestions!

Franchisee

The typical franchisee wants to earn a respectable income—without having a boss along with it—by taking advantage of someone else's turnkey idea. And that must take place in a no-risk environment. Since most franchisees are really "buying a job" rather than going into business for themselves in the traditional sense, they don't represent the popular model of the entrepreneur.

The average franchisee is not only willing to take advice

and heed external guidance, but usually actively seeks it out.

When you're looking to earn referrals to franchisees, it's important to highlight independence and predictability.

On the Phone

You say: When I'm working with my clients, I prefer to help them maintain their personal independence. [Our product/ service] is dependable and operates the same way every day. Clients choose to work with us over and over because we're steady and reliable. We help our clients take the risk out of decision making. And we do it all at a prudent price. Can you think of someone who might be interested in meeting some- one like me?

Face-to-Face

You say: I'd prefer to work with clients who enjoy being in charge and are looking for an accepted, debugged, and dependable [product/service] that comes from a steady and reliable provider like us. Our clients turn to us because we help them take the risk out of decision making. And our price is always sensible. With that kind of explanation, who comes to mind?

E-Mail

You write: Can you think of anyone I might be able to meet who is interested in our turnkey solutions that would help them maintain their personal independence? Our respected [product/service] is popular because it runs the same way every day. We are always available to our clients so we can help them take the risk out of decision making. Can you think of anyone who might be looking for a supplier like that? I'll follow up by phone in a few days to learn more about whom you have in mind.

Social Media

You post: Our proven [product/service] helps ensure my clients are in charge of their own businesses. Message me with suggested contacts!

Hematologist

Hematologists are probably the most secure of any of the major medical specialists. They've managed to carve out comfortable niches for themselves. They do a specialized kind of work that places them safely out of the way of the hospitals' political infighting.

Compared with the other specialists, most hematologists have limited patient lists. Their roles are to act as diagnostic tools for the attending or referring physicians. Specifically, hematologists analyze the patients' blood and design therapies to cure whatever pathologies they find.

In diagnosing diseases of the blood and designing the appropriate therapy, the hematologist isn't going into areas where there are great unsolved riddles and challenges.

With all this security comes a lot of peace and quiet. As a result, when seeking referrals to hematologists, talk about your ability to keep calm and do what's expected.

On the Phone

You say: I work with hematologists who don't let anyone rock the boat. That's because [our product/service] is up-to-date and covers all the bases it's supposed to cover. After all, my clients don't need people who bring stress into their lives. They need someone who will do their homework and doesn't jump to conclusions. And that's exactly how I operate. In fact,

I'm often told that our clients like working with us because of the stress-free way we quietly operate. And we do it all at a reasonable price. With that explanation, can you think of someone who might benefit from working with me?

Face-to-Face

You say: I'm hoping to meet more hematologists I can work with. Specifically, I'd like to work with people who want to work at their own pace to keep doing what satisfies them. [Our product/service] performs for our clients without any headaches and won't cut into the time that's important to them. Our company is made up of people who are dedicated to taking the time to do their homework. We work hard to maintain peace and quiet on behalf of our clients. And our prices don't violate good judgment. With that description, can you think of any hematologists I might meet?

E-Mail

You write: I'm hoping to meet hematologists I might be able to serve; however, I don't want to ask them to fix what isn't broken. Instead, I'll take my time to do my homework to understand whether we can perform for them without any headaches. After all, they don't need me to bring stress into their lives. [Our product/service] is stress free and quiet. Can you think of anyone who might benefit? I'll give you a call in the next one or two days to talk about whom you have in mind.

Social Media

You post: Never change something that works! [Our product/service] performs for my hematologist clients without any headaches. Do you know anyone I can serve?

Hospital Administrator

The typical hospital administrator wants maximum personal visibility within the healthcare industry, which he perceives is only possible by having significant operational control over the hospital. The administrator of a 200-bed hospital has no higher career goals to satisfy at that institution. She can only advance by moving to a 500-bed hospital. And once that goal is accomplished, there's nowhere to go but out and up again. So, it's on to a 1,000-bed hospital.

So, hospital administrators perceive that they must protect their careers from less budget-conscious team members. That means administrators have to maintain control because they're convinced that there are few others who can be trusted with decisions related to finances.

When you're seeking referrals to hospital administrators, it's important to highlight your understanding of these decision makers' needs for control.

On the Phone

You say: In my work with hospital administrators, I've found the hospitals that run best are those where the administrator is in control. That's why I try to work with my clients in a way that supports their control so they can get results that impress the people who are watching them. [Our product/service] is adaptable to all kinds of challenges and has a reasonable life cost. Our company is sensitive to business requirements and it helps our clients see success on a large scale. We do this in such a way that makes a high return on investment possible. Can you think of any hospital administrators whom I could meet?

Face-to-Face

You say: I'm hoping you might be able to introduce me to some hospital administrators to help me grow my business. I prefer to work with people who take control and keep it, and who understand that the world pays attention to people who get results. [Our product/service] is responsive to change. Everyone at our company understands what our clients' priorities are, which allows us to help them impress the right people and remain at the forefront with the people who matter. And we do it with a favorable economic impact. With that said, can you think of any hospital administrators who might enjoy meeting me?

E-Mail

You write: I help hospital administrators move in the directions they want to go by enabling them to get results that impress the people who are watching. [Our product/service] is adaptable to all kinds of challenges, and our company is sensitive to business requirements. We help our clients gain significant success. Can you think of any hospital administrators I might meet? I'll give you a call tomorrow to discuss whom you have in mind.

Social Media

You post: Hospitals that run the best are those where the administrator is in control. [Our product/service] enables that to happen. Help me meet more hospital administrators to serve!

Hospital Materials Manager

Hospital materials managers want to maintain their decision-making authority to hold on to their places in the hospital's power structure. The average materials manager didn't get there by going to medical school or by studying hospital administration in a prestigious university. She got there by starting as a "tech," working up through the ranks to radiology administrator or chief technician, and eventually, becoming a materials manager.

We've observed that the materials manager is often an internal advocate for salespeople by championing the product or service within the hospital, by guiding the salesperson around the bureaucratic obstacles, and by helping the salesperson avoid fatal mistakes.

When it comes to earning referrals to hospital materials managers, show how you help them maintain control in areas where they can be important members of a team.

On the Phone

You say: When it comes to working with my clients, I like to help them keep tight control over everything that goes on around them so they don't let things get out of hand. [Our product/service] offers a favorable economic impact and is well thought out and user friendly. We don't believe in cutting corners or playing games, which means we watch out for the hospitals' interests. Finally, there's a good return on investment. With that explanation, can you think of any hospital materials managers you know?

Face-to-Face

You say: I'm hoping you can introduce me to hospital materials managers. Specifically, I'd like to meet those who don't let things get out of hand and are valuable members of their teams. [Our product/service] well provides them because it's easy to understand and doesn't require a lot of study. Our company is made up of straightforward people who help our clients protect the hospitals. We price everything so that there are solid returns. Who comes to mind?

E-Mail

You write: Can you introduce me to any hospital materials managers who keep tight control over everything that goes on around them? Our [product/service] has a favorable economic impact, which means our clients don't have to defend or apologize for their decisions. We don't play games; we watch out for the hospitals' interests. Can you think of anyone who might enjoy meeting me? If so, let me know. I'll follow up by phone early next week.

Social Media

You post: I don't let my clients allow things to get out of hand because they never have to defend their decisions to use our [product/service]. Can you think of any hospital materials managers I can meet?

Human Resources Training Executive

The typical human resources training executive wants to be considered by senior management as worthy of the same kind of respect, recognition, and self-validation that management receives.

Some providers claim that many HR training executives are so concerned with price that they seem to place little value on quality. Quality doesn't seem to overcome price sensitivity. Many HR training executives are known for their almost single-minded focus on price. And it's a common belief that HR training executives are often ordered to buy at the lowest available price.

When you're seeking referrals to HR training executives, show them that you recognize the important roles they play in the organizations and how your offering would fit in well with everything they're already doing without creating additional work.

On the Phone

You say: In my work with HR training executives, I've found that they probably do a lot more than they get credit for. Our [product/service] fits right in with what they're doing and adds to what they've already done. It's designed to be easily adaptable to their purposes. Our people are dependable and relationship oriented. They help our clients get their points across more persuasively. And our prices are directly related to the benefits. Can you think of any HR training executives who might enjoy working with someone like me?

Face-to-Face

You say: I've found that HR training executives do important work and make big contributions to their companies' success. And I like to work with my clients in a way that supports their efforts. Our [product/service] builds on what our clients have already accomplished and we give them control over the outcome. Our people are loyal and serve as our clients' external support staff. Our clients tell us that they hire us because we accept them for who they are and what they do. Our prices are justified by the benefits. Now, who comes to mind?

E-Mail

You write: Our HR training executive clients probably do a lot more than they get credit for. That's why we support the big contributions they're already making. Our [product/service] easily adapts to their purposes and adds to what they already have. Our people are interactive and loyal. Can you think of any HR training executives I could meet? I'll give you a call later this week to discuss whom you have in mind.

Social Media

You post: We help HR training executives gain respect for the important work they do. Do you know anyone we can help?

Insurance Claims Adjuster

The word *undemanding* describes the adjuster's ideal work environment. It doesn't mean that demands are completely absent, but that whatever demands happen to exist can be satisfied with relative ease. The adjuster's role is predictable. He or she generally performs the same routine functions, day in and day out. Consistent expectations and performance pressure may be a daily occurrence.

When you're attempting to earn referrals from decision makers like this one, it's important to highlight your ability to help relieve burdens and pressures they may face.

On the Phone

You say: When I work with my adjuster clients, I prefer to help them take the load off themselves. There's nothing complex about our [product/service]. It's easy to understand and practical. We work hard to ensure that we have hassle-free relationships with our clients and that our prices are justifiable. Knowing that about me, what adjusters come to mind?

Face-to-Face

You say: I'm hoping you might be able to introduce me to adjusters whom I can serve. Specifically, I'm looking to meet adjusters who have reasonable goals and want to take the pressure off. I work well with those types of adjusters because I stay out of the ivory tower and our [product/service] is practical and not based on theory. Because we believe fighting never solved anything, we don't believe in starting arguments. We provide competitive estimates and valuations. With that explanation, who comes to mind?

E-Mail

You write: Can you introduce me to any insurance claims adjusters who prefer undemanding environments? Our [product/service] well provides them because it's not abstract. Our company is made up of reasonable people. Our clients are never stuck in the middle. Can you think of any adjusters who might enjoy working with someone like me? If so, let me know. I'll follow up by phone by the end of this week.

Social Media

You post: I help take the load off insurance claims adjusters and put the pressure where it belongs. Message me if you know of any adjusters I should meet.

Medical/Dental Office Manager

This decision maker wants to be the favorite and most trusted member of a team that serves an authority figure. The medical practice office manager wants to have a relationship with an authority figure, like the physician or dentist, that gives him or her what we call *reflected validation*.

Office managers have a strong need for approval from people who are in higher positions than their own. The reason has to do with career success. They feel that they'll succeed in direct proportion to how closely they can identify themselves with the person who's in charge . . . assuming, of course, that the person in charge is powerful and respected.

That's what we mean when we say that office managers seek reflected validation. In other words, the perception is that the power and prestige of the authority figure will reflect well

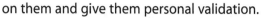

on them and give them personal validation.

When you're trying to earn referrals to medical or dental office managers, emphasize your understanding of this fact. Highlight your respect for their abilities to keep everything on track and organized.

On the Phone

You say: Are you able to introduce me to any medical/dental office managers? When I work with my clients, I recognize that they keep everything on track, no matter what comes at them. That's important because they won't have to spend hours studying our [product/service] before they can understand how to use it. We never put our clients under the gun because we appreciate what they're going through. After all, they've earned the right to have people pay attention to them. And they won't get an argument from the doctor over our price. Can you think of any medical/dental office managers I should meet?

Face-to-Face

You say: I'd like to meet medical/dental office managers who make sure everyone gets what they need. Our [product/service] is for the person who's in the middle of everything. We pay attention to what they have to say because we understand what they're going through. After all, they've paid their dues and have earned the rights to have people pay attention to what they have to say. And our [product/service] is easy to get approval for. Can you think of any medical/dental office managers I can meet?

E-Mail

You write: Can you help me meet any medical/dental office managers? Specifically, I'm looking to meet those in offices where approval goes through them, and everyone depends on them. Those office managers are the kinds of people who benefit most from our [product/service] because it's for the people who are in the middle of everything. Does anyone come to mind? If so, let me know. I'll follow up by phone in a few days.

Social Media

You post: Looking to help more medical/dental office managers who keep everything on track, no matter what comes at them. Message me with suggestions!

Oncologist

The typical oncologist wants to make extraordinary discoveries that haven't already been made and achieve unprecedented breakthroughs in a high-risk environment.

When you're trying to earn referrals to this decision maker, it's important to emphasize your appreciation of her ability to be out in front.

On the Phone

You say: I'm hoping you might be able to introduce me to oncologists I can work with. Specifically, I'm looking for those doctors who are out in front, constantly breaking new ground, and making extraordinary discoveries. Our [product/service] can serve them well because it's up-to-date and is beyond question. We stand behind our [product/service] and are constantly acquiring more and more information, which we share with our customers. We are committed to staying on the cutting edge. Our prices are easily justified. Can you think of anyone who might be interested in meeting with me?

Face-to-Face

You say: Do you know of any oncologists who are out in front, seeking extraordinary discoveries? Our [product/service] well provides them with its unimpeachable data and its place in accepted protocols. We understand how they want the relationships with a provider like us to work so we support their intellectual curiosities. Our company is recognized for being in the lead. And our price won't upset the administrator, CFO, or materials manager. With that introduction, can you think of anyone I might be able to meet?

E-Mail

You write: Do you know any oncologists who are making major impacts in their field? I'd like to meet doctors who never hang back. We share our [product/service] with our clients because we know they're intellectually curious. Given that introduction, can you think of anyone who might enjoy meeting with me? I'll give you a call in the next one or two days so we can discuss this further.

Social Media

You post: I help oncologists remain out in front with our [product/service]. Please message me if you know of anyone I should meet.

Pathologist

Hospital pathologists want to be treated as the equals of other diagnosticians. In many cases, they also want to assimilate successfully into the hospital environment.

A pathologist looks at a slide, finds a single cell, and matches it to the appropriate disease.

When you're attempting to earn referrals to this type of decision maker, be sure to emphasize the fact that he is a vital player in the hospital's infrastructure.

On the Phone

You say: Can you think of any pathologists I might be able to meet? They're important because the hospital couldn't get along without their services. Pathologists like our [product/service] because it's fast and easy to use. Even so, we are meticulous and careful about everything we do. And that means we're predictable and stress free. Our price justifies itself. Who comes to mind?

Face-to-Face

You say: I'm hoping you can introduce me to any pathologists you know. I enjoy working with them because so many professionals depend on them. Our [product/service] helps them prevent costly mistakes. It's easy to use and helps take the pressure off. Our clients tell us they enjoy working with us because of our patience. We always provide reproducible results at a price that defies argument. Can you think of anyone with whom I could meet?

NONCLIENT PHRASES ←

E-Mail

You write: I work with pathologists who understand that the hospitals couldn't get along without their services. They like our [product/service] because of its precision and ease of use. We are careful about everything we do and never rush. We're often chosen because of our predictability and stress-free way of doing business. Can you think of anyone I should meet? If so, let me know. I'll give you a call by the end of the week to talk about whom you have in mind.

Social Media

You post: The hospital couldn't get along without a pathologist's services. Do you know any I can help with our [product/service]?

Primary Care Physician

The central issue in this decision maker's professional life is the freedom of the independent agent. Primary care physicians don't like bureaucracies, paperwork, regulations, or anything else that's associated with corporate medicine.

By going into private practice, rather than working for an institution, the primary care physician is expressing the need to be his or her own person not only as a physician, but as an *entrepreneurial* physician.

To earn referrals to primary care physicians, be sure to mention your understanding of the importance of freedom and independence.

On the Phone

You say: I work with primary care physicians who value independence and practicing medicine instead of pushing paper. Our [product/service] doesn't require extraordinary attention. It doesn't take them away from the practice of medicine. Our company values our clients' expertise, so we offer simple, straightforward answers. Our price is directly related to the value we offer. With that in mind, can you think of any primary care physicians you can introduce me to?

Face-to-Face

You say: Can you introduce me to any primary care physicians? Specifically, I'm looking for those who want to practice their art without outside interference. Our [product/service] is easy to use and doesn't get in the way. Our company has simple, straightforward answers, and none of us believes there's any substitute for honesty. We work with our clients in ways that reduce outside interference because we have a lot of empathy for their situation. It's easy to translate the cost of our [product/service] into value. Given that explanation, who comes to mind?

E-Mail

You write: Do you know of any primary care physicians I can meet? I'd like to work with the doctors who are fulfilling the reasons they went to medical school. After all, they didn't go to medical school to become office managers! Our [product/service] is easy to use and everyone in our company has simple, straightforward answers. Further, it reduces outside interference. With that said, can you think of anyone I can meet? I'll follow up by phone in a few days to discuss whom you have in mind.

Social Media

You post: Primary care physicians should be able to exercise their independence and professional discretion. That's how I work with my clients. If you know of anyone I should meet, please message me!

Process Engineer

The process engineer usually considers himself to be superior to the other members of the team, especially in high-tech manufacturing environments, such as semiconductor "fabs." Specifically, process engineers think of superiority as a function of whether one's work is abstract or concrete. The more abstract it is, the more superior one is supposed to be. Thus, most process engineers consider their work to be highly abstract and theoretical.

In comparison with equipment engineers, for example, process engineers deal with intangibles. They don't do the kinds of hands-on work the equipment engineers do because the idea of the process itself is an abstraction. They deal in theories, models, and a number of other things you can't literally touch.

When you're attempting to earn referrals to this type of decision maker, don't fail to mention the difficult and intellectually challenging work she does.

On the Phone

You say: When I work with my process engineer clients, I recognize that they're doing difficult work and others should follow their lead. Our [product/service] well provides them because it's state of the art. Our company is process oriented, and we know how the parts fit into the whole. That's important because process requirement should be uppermost. Everything we do is at a justifiable price. What process engineers come to mind when I describe the work I do?

Face-to-Face

You say: Do you know of any process engineers I could meet? Specifically, I'm looking to meet those who are leaders or first among equals. Because our [product/service] is cutting edge, it's the kind only a few can appreciate and understand. We understand the things that are important to our clients, so we're driven by engineering priorities. And, at the end of the day, nothing should get in the way of the process. Everything we do is at a price no one can challenge. Can you think of any process engineers I can meet?

E-Mail

You write: I like to work with process engineers who are in leadership positions because our [product/service] is a real innovation. Everyone in our company has an engineering mentality and none of us believes anything should get in the way of the process. Can you think of anyone I should meet? I'll give you a call in a day or two to talk about this some more.

Social Media

You post: Looking to link up with leaders among process engineers. Whom should I reach out to?

Purchasing Agent/Manager

The typical purchasing agent wants to be considered by senior management as worthy of the same kind of respect, recognition, and self-validation that senior management receives.

User groups rarely take the time to inform purchasing agents of anything but the most rudimentary facts, and users only transfer real buying authority to the purchasing department on issues of no perceived importance. "If it meets the specs, I don't care whom you buy it from" is an expression purchasing agents report hearing frequently from their users.

It's not unusual for purchasing agents to be perceived by vendors as excessively demanding and even unreasonable. Specifically, vendors may claim that many purchasing agents are so obsessively concerned with price that they seem to place little value on quality. Quality doesn't seem to overcome price sensitivity.

However, more than 62 percent of the purchasing agents studied in so-called "lowest-price" environments admit to legally adjusting their specifications or calculations to award favored vendors whose prices aren't the lowest. The more typical revisions have to do with the calculation of issues such as useful product life, anticipated benefits, compatibility, upgradability, and a number of other factors that could complicate the issue of price.

When it comes to earning referrals with this type of decision maker, be sure to talk about how much respect you have for him and your understanding of the fact that he deserves more credit than he's given.

On the Phone

You say: I recognize that purchasing agents probably do a lot more than they get credit for. After all, they're making a big contribution to their companies. Our [product/service] is a safe purchase that's easy to understand. Our company is patient and interested in our customers. We believe things should run smoothly for the purchasing agents we work with. And our price is directly related to the benefits we provide. With that introduction, can you think of any purchasing agents I should meet?

Face-to-Face

You say: I'd like to find more purchasing agents to serve. Do you know of any who are making big contributions to their companies, but might not be getting the credit or respect they deserve? Because our [product/service] is a safe purchase that doesn't require a lot of technical education, it serves them well. Our company is patient and we don't attach any strings to the relationships with them. We don't create any crises because things should run smoothly for our clients. Our price is always justified by the benefits. Who comes to mind?

E-Mail

You write: Do you know of any purchasing agents I can meet? Specifically, I'm looking for anyone who is making a big contribution to her company, but might not be getting the credit or respect she deserves. Our [product/service] is not technically challenging and our people ensure that things run smoothly for our clients. Let me know who comes to mind. I'll give you a call in a few days to discuss this further.

Social Media

You post: Purchasing agents make big contributions, but don't always get the credit they deserve. I can help. Message me if you think of anyone I can serve.

Radiologist

Most hospital radiologists want to regain the power and prestige the specialty of radiology lost when conditions changed in the healthcare industry. For many years, a radiologist could get whatever diagnostic tool he or she wanted. Over time, the MRI became the tool of choice of the radiologist. However, because it is so expensive, purchasing an MRI scanner is now a committee decision.

Suddenly, the CFO, the materials manager, and the hospital administrator began exercising their authority. Radiologists had to consider issues such as return on investment and equipment financing, which used to be the concern only of the hospital administrator and the CFO.

Now, it's common for radiologists to feel less influential in their hospitals. Therefore, when you're attempting to earn referrals to radiologists, be sure to emphasize the critical roles they play at the center of everything that happens.

On the Phone

You say: I'm hoping you can introduce me to some radiologists. When I've been working with them I've found that they're right at the center of everything. Our [product/service] well provides them because it's ahead of the development curve and won't turn them into manual laborers. Our company is made up of strong innovators and we offer the best support available. When we're working with our radiologist clients, we help them take the leads and hold them. We do all of this at an easily justified price. With that in mind, can you think of any radiologists I should meet?

Face-to-Face

You say: Can you think of any radiologists I can meet? Because they often have the most riding on their decisions, our [product/service] provides them well. It performs for them to its full potential and is easy to manage. Our company has a first-class reputation for being a strong innovator. We also believe our clients are the best qualified to be in charge, so we defer to them in that way. And, of course, our price is easily justifiable. With that explanation, who comes to mind?

E-Mail

You write: For my radiologist clients, their art is more important than mere numbers. In fact, without them and their art, the hospital would come to a grinding halt. I'm hoping you can introduce me to some more radiologists because our [product/service] is easy to manage and doesn't force them to do the things they don't want to do. We provide them with the best support available so they can control the important decisions. Who comes to mind when you hear about how I like to do business? I'll give you a call next week to talk about this.

Social Media

You post: Radiologists are right at the center of everything, which is why they benefit from our state-of-the-art [product/service]. Message me if you know of someone I should meet!

Real Estate Manager

The real estate manager wants to be insulated from risk to a far greater degree than almost any other manager in the company, even including the CFO.

One of the risks that is most ominous for this decision maker is the risk associated with change. The real estate manager's perception is that change brings with it unpredictability, and unpredictability is something this decision maker does not want to experience.

When you're trying to earn referrals to this type of decision maker, discuss your understanding of his need for comfort and steadiness.

On the Phone

You say: I'm hoping you can introduce me to real estate managers who want to be comfortable with whatever comes along. Our [product/service] is reliable and makes change work for them. Our company takes a cautious approach so everything stays under control. Clients hire us over and over because we are calm and preserve our clients' integrity. And we do it all at a textbook price. With that introduction, who comes to mind?

Face-to-Face

You say: Can you introduce me to real estate managers? I know they work to protect themselves so they are comfortable with whatever comes along. And I work well with them because our [product/service] is predictable and has a large customer/client/installed base. Our company believes we should not be in a big hurry. Instead, we should get to know our potential clients over a period of time. We want to help our clients take advantage of opportunities with no outside interference. We do this at a textbook price. Given that context, who comes to mind?

E-Mail

You write: Do you know of any real estate managers I can help? Our [product/service] is reliable and makes change work for them. We take a cautious approach and get to know our prospective clients over a period of time. This calm advancement preserves our clients' integrity. Can you think of anyone who might be interested in meeting someone like me? I'll follow up by phone in a day or two to discuss whom you have in mind.

Social Media

You post: Real estate managers can turn change to their advantages. Ask me how!

Researcher

The typical researcher wants to make a discovery and to get sole credit for it. That discovery has to represent dramatic progress because the researcher is often out to make history.

Many decision makers are reluctant to incur risks. But most researchers are actually attracted to them because they present them with the opportunities to gain satisfying results that they couldn't get without taking the risks. Those satisfying results are, of course, discoveries of substantial importance.

What the specific discovery happens to be depends on the researcher's particular industry and application. A researcher working in the classic R&D commercial environment, for example, is searching for the product or service design no one else has yet developed. In the more traditional research situation, the objective might be anything from data to a formula to a new drug.

When you're attempting to earn referrals to this type of decision maker, it's important to mention your appreciation of his role out in front, along with his need to get things right.

On the Phone

You say: I'm hoping you can introduce me to any researchers you might know. I'd especially like to meet anyone you know who is far from the ivory tower and moving past what is already known. Our [product/service] is exceptionally accurate and adaptable, and it keeps up with our clients at their own speed. Our company provides support whenever our clients need it, and we're not willing to live with shortcuts. Our clients hire us over and over because we help them generate results that are convincing beyond any doubt. And our prices never go over the line. With that introduction, who comes to mind?

Face-to-Face

You say: Can you think of any researchers you might be able to introduce me to? Specifically, I'd like to meet anyone who has a strong reputation for breaking new ground. That's because our [product/service] is not the usual solution. It won't distract her and is truly extraordinary. Our company won't compromise the truth, and our people are intellectually curious. We're hired for our precision and convincing conclusions. And there's nothing extravagant about our prices. Who comes to mind?

E-Mail

You write: I hope to meet researchers who are doing groundbreaking work and are looking for a [product/service] provider with nothing less than extraordinary support and no patience for compromises. We're hired for our precision and abilities to make things happen in the world. With that introduction, can you think of anyone I can meet? I'll call you tomorrow to talk about whom you have in mind.

Social Media

You post: Our [product/service] won't distract you because it's adaptable and has a fast turn-around time. Message me if you know of any researchers who would like to learn more!

Semiconductor "Fab" Manager

Fab managers are, of course, the people "at the top of the fab pyramid." From that vantage point, they have the perspectives of being the "businesspeople" of the group. Of all the decision-maker types who work in semiconductor environments and are involved in the buying decisions, fab managers are the most sensitive to the result of the fab process.

At the same time, fab managers are less sensitive to its inner workings than the other team members are. In fact, their backgrounds are just as likely to be in finance or marketing as in more technical applications. In view of the priorities of their positions, they're concerned about having bottom lines. For them, the relevant issues are costs, budgets, and safety.

Thus, if the fab achieves a certain level of yield that is pronounced acceptable by their superiors, most fab managers will be reluctant to tamper with it, even if some legitimate improvements are within reach. Although not totally unwilling to pursue those improvements, they're more inclined to leave well enough alone, if that can be justified.

When you're trying to earn referrals to this type of decision maker, highlight this knowledge.

On the Phone

You say: Are you able to introduce me to any fab managers? Specifically, I'm looking for the people who are staying out of the spotlight and believe that, if it isn't broken, it shouldn't be fixed. Our [product/service] integrates smoothly into the fab and is reliable. Companies hire us because we're operationally sound. We keep the process in perspective, but aren't obsessed with it. We operate quietly and without incident. Our price is justified by what's at stake. Knowing that, who comes to mind?

Face-to-Face

You say: Can you introduce me to any fab managers? I'm looking to meet people who want to stay in control without having to be hands on. Our [product/service] is reliable and not a disruption. Our company doesn't get carried away with our own [product/service]. We're financially stable and operationally sound. We help our clients operate quietly and without incident. Our price is consistent with the stakes. With that in mind, can you think of anyone I should meet?

E-Mail

You write: I'm hoping you might know some fab managers you can introduce me to. I would like to meet people who place safety at the forefront of everything they do and can stay in control without having to be hands on. Our [product/service] integrates smoothly into the fab, which has been proven by our large installed base. With that said, can you think of anyone who might like to meet with me? If so, let me know. I'll follow up with you by phone in a few days to talk about this more.

Social Media

You post: I help fab managers meet precision, budget, and safety standards behind the scenes. If you know of any fab managers looking for [product/service], please message me!

Surgeon

Surgeons want acknowledgment of their positions as one of the most important members of the therapeutic team. From the surgeon's perspective, everyone else—the array of technicians, orderlies, and so on—are just part of the rank-and-file who keep the hospital running so the surgeon can continue to practice his art.

There's a pecking order among surgeons, too. The closer you operate to what's considered a vital organ, the more prestige you have. The lowest ranking member in the pecking order is often the cosmetic surgeon. Ironically, cosmetic surgeons often earn bigger incomes than most of the other surgical specialists. But money isn't the deciding factor in the pecking order—prestige is.

When you're trying to earn referrals to this type of decision maker, emphasize your understanding of her prestigious position in the pecking order.

On the Phone

You say: Can you introduce me to any surgeons? I'm best able to help those who are out in front, showing the paths for others to follow. That's because our [product/service] is prestigious and highly regarded. Our company is selected because we perform well under difficult conditions and minimize complications. Our price is easily justified. Can you think of any surgeons who might enjoy the chance to meet with me?

Face-to-Face

You say: When I work with surgeons, I prefer to do so in a way that helps them fulfill the most important role. They really are holding the patient's welfare in their hands and our [product/service] supports them when they do because it's easy to use and contributes to quick action. Our company is supportive and ready to turn around and respond at a moment's notice. On top of that, our price is one that won't upset the administrator, the CFO, or the materials manager. So, given that introduction, can you think of any surgeons I might be able to help?

E-Mail

You write: I'd like to meet surgeons who take leadership positions and are right on the front lines. Our [product/service] is prestigious and elite. Our company is supportive and quick acting. Given that introduction, can you think of anyone I should meet? If so, let me know. I'll give you a call next week to discuss whom you have in mind.

Social Media

You post: I help surgeons who light the paths for the others to follow who take leadership positions. If you can think of any surgeons I should meet, please message me!

CHAPTER 9

Getting Recommendations

Even when you're selling to a referral, you need to justify the claims you make about your offering. After all, your prospects expect you to make claims about your products and services. But they're surprised when they hear those claims endorsed by third parties. An important step is to solicit recommendations, testimonial letters, and references.

Once you earn these indispensable sources of social proof, use them with referrals and other nonclients to enhance your value—the value of your solution. In this chapter, we look at the phrases to use to earn some of that social proof. We also look at strategies to use to apply these resources in several situations. You'll notice that G2G still applies: To get this kind of social proof, you must provide value to the people you're asking to help.

Social proof is any third-party corroboration of your claims. Often it comes from testimonials; however, if you're living the G2G philosophy, your strongest social proof comes from the fact that your relationships are built on referrals.

Using Social Proof for Maximum Impact

After making a sales presentation to a referral, it's smart to check in by asking something like:

You say: As you recall, [name of connector] introduced us to one another because [he/she] thought we would be able to help you. It looks like we can. Would it be helpful for you to reconnect with [name of connector]?

or

You say: What else can I show you at this point that might help you make a decision? For example, would you like to speak with someone we've worked with who has successfully solved a problem similar to yours?

Alternatively, once you have adequately presented your product or service, created great value for it, and ensured your presentation was 100 percent on target for your prospect, here's the next step.

You say: Now, let me show you what other [people or organizations] like you have to say about our [product/service/company/warranty/delivery/etc.].

At this point, consider offering one or more of three ways for your prospect to experience corroboration of your claims.

For example, if your prospect shows concern or disbelief over quality or product claims you have made:

You say: Let me show what [title], the leading trade journal in your industry, has to say about our quality.

or

You say: Let me show you how we rank in the latest research by *Consumer Reports* [or some other relevant, respected, third-party evaluation].

Put the hard copy of the report data directly in their hands. Let them read it for themselves. Then you follow up:

You say: Can you see why we're so highly rated by those who research and rank [products/services] like ours?

If your prospect shows concern over the credibility of your statements:

You say: Let me show you some letters we've received from several people we do business with, [people/companies] like [you/yours].

    or

You say: Let me show you some testimonials on our website that we've received from several people we do business with, [people/companies] like [you/yours].

At this point, show them letters or website testimonials from satisfied users of your product or service that you've prepared that corroborate your claims. Allow them to read, touch, and keep these letters. Highlight key phrases, if possible. The most influential social proof can often be a testimonial from the connector. Then you follow up:

You say: Hopefully you can see the client's positive reaction to what we provide. Do these comments satisfy any concern you have relative to [quality/delivery/service/price/etc.]?

There are three possibilities:

You hear: Yes, it does.

You have moved one step closer to the sale. In fact, you may want to take a closing action at this point.

    or

You hear: No, not really.

or

You hear: I'm not sure.

If the prospect is not satisfied, proceed to the next level:

You say: Would you like to directly speak with one of our satisfied [customers/clients]? That way you can pose your question or have your concern answered personally by someone who, clearly, has nothing to gain. If that's what you'd prefer to do, here is a list of [six is an ideal number] people who have agreed to talk with anyone like you who might have a question. Would you like to do that?

Two possibilities:

You hear: Yes, I would.

You say: That's great. Is there a person, or several people, on the list whom you'd prefer to call? The reason I'm asking is that I want to be sure to alert them to expect your call. We do this as a courtesy to them so they can anticipate the conversation and be prepared for it. Is that okay with you?

You hear: That's fine.

You say: Do you have any idea when you might be calling them so I can give them an indication as to the timing?

You hear: Within the next week or so.

You say: Good. Now, which clients do you prefer to call?

Once you have determined who will be called and when, you continue:

You say: You should have all of your calls completed by [date]. Is that correct? Would you prefer that I call you a day or so after that, or should I wait for your call?

Get an answer. In either case, you need to move closer to finalizing the sale.

or

You hear: No, that's not necessary.

You may want to do one of two things.

You say: OK, then, does everything look acceptable to you?

or

You say: What further evidence, if any, do you need to move ahead?

In either case, you are now forcing your prospect's hand. You will determine if he or she is prepared to buy, is stalling, or needs more evidence.

We consider a third possibility in a moment.

If it seems the prospect is prepared to buy or is stalling, you need to move to finalize the sale. Here's how you determine whether the prospect is prepared to buy.

You say: Why do you say that?

Two possibilities:

You hear: I'm ready to move ahead.

At this point it's time to take a closing action.

or

You hear: I would rather find out for myself.

You say: Would you like to experience the [product/service] yourself?

You hear: Yes, I would.

You say: We have lots of [customers/clients] who like to do that. When that's the case, we often run trials, beta tests, or offer demonstrations. [Name of connector] actually demoed a [similar product/service you're recommending] as part of their decision-making process. Let me tell you how that works.

Set up the test and determine what parameters will be used to define success. Assume once those parameters have been met, it's time for you to ask for the commitment.

Getting Satisfied Customers to Help You Sell

In the real world of selling, lots of clients or customers will readily agree to have their names on a list to be contacted if you ask them to. Those eager enough to do it on their own are few and far between. And how do you ask customers to indicate their level of satisfaction with your product or service?

Some people will not offer to help but will help you if you ask them. To more fully and carefully prepare the tools you'll need to convince your prospects your claims are true, you need to know how to secure words of approval from your satisfied customers.

Let's talk about what to say, when to say it, and how to secure the testimonials. You need one or more of basically three types:

1. Evidence of satisfaction such as a letter, audio, or video testimonial
2. A satisfied client's name, contact information, and type of product or service provided, to be placed on a list agreeing to be called
3. A willingness to supply you with the name and information you'll need to make contact with potential prospects

The ideal time to approach someone about this is easy to

understand. It's when you have earned the right to do so. Period. However, there is one exception to that rule. When your customer says, "You're really great!" or something to that effect, take advantage of that opportunity—even if you believe that you have more work to do to feel you have fully satisfied them. The real truth? They must be satisfied enough to verbalize their pleasure. That's all.

Compiling References

A smart strategy is to have a prepared list of happy, satisfied customers whom prospects can contact if they choose. These are different than your connectors, but they are still a highly influential resource for gaining new business. They're people who are willing to hear from prospects when those prospects need to have questions answered. Here's how to secure those who are most willing to be on the list.

You say: Would you mind if I placed your name, contact information, and type of [product/service] we provided to you on a list for other prospective customers to review?

There are two possibilities:

You hear: Yes, that's okay with me.

You say: I will promise you this. If anyone does want to contact you, I will tell him that, as a matter of courtesy to you, I will inform you so you will be able to anticipate his call. Does all of this sound okay?

You hear: That's fine.

You say: Good. I also promise that I'll only keep your name on the list for a short time. That way you won't have to worry about it. In fact, I'll even contact you when it's time for me to remove you from the list. What do you think?

or

You hear: No, I don't want to do that.

You say: I understand. However, is there any specific reason why you wouldn't be interested?

Based on the response, you may want to either resolve the concern or get your customer to agree to write a letter of recommendation. This is an opportunity to uncover any problems an otherwise happy customer has with your [product/service].

If the initial response to your request is negative, consider this approach:

You say: That's fine, I understand. However, if someone does want to talk with you, is that okay?

Then proceed accordingly.

Many prospects will ask for a list and never call anyone. They only want to be sure you have a list of satisfied customers. However, in today's rapidly changing economic climate, reference checks have become more important than ever. What used to be an atypical practice has become a regular and consistent one.

So when a prospect indicates that he or she will contact someone, you do need to get in touch with your customer and inform him or her that a prospect will probably call. Often, you can e-mail your customer of the possible call. However, if you choose to make a phone call, here's how that conversation usually goes:

You say: Hello, Terry. This is _____. How are you?

You hear: Hi, _____. How are you?

You say: I'm great. The reason for my call is that one of our prospective customers, Bob Jones with XYZ Corporation, indicated that he'd like to talk with you. Is that OK?

Here's the most interesting part. If you have placed highly satisfied customers on the list, they will ask you this simple, straightforward question nearly 100 percent of the time:

You hear: What do you want me to say?

Your answer? Tell them to answer truthfully, of course, and to frame their response within the context of how you want to help your prospect address a need, handle a problem, or overcome an objection. Or, your prospect wants corroboration of your claims from an independent third party—your happy, satisfied customer. And your customers will do that, as long as you have earned the right for them to be totally enthusiastic about you, your product or service, and your organization.

Other Types of Social Proof

Beyond asking for a reference, there are a number of other ways to leverage satisfied clients.

Testimonial Letters

Testimonial letters are valuable tools to share with prospective clients. One of the best ways to use them is to identify an objection that prospects commonly express and find an existing client who had the same concern, but worked with you anyway. Ask the satisfied customer to write a letter that features the process he or she followed to overcome the objection. When talking with the existing customer about the testimonial letter:

You say: When you first began discussing the idea of working with us, you expressed some concern about the size of our organization. Now that we've been working together for several months, do you still have that concern?

You hear: No. You've shown yourselves to be very adaptable to our requests.

You say: As you can imagine, you're not the only person who has raised that concern during the buying process. Would you be willing to write a letter about that concern and how you moved beyond it?

You hear: Sure.

You say: Great! Knowing how busy you are, would it be helpful for me to put together some bullet points or even a few paragraphs that you can edit as you'd like?

You hear: That would be great.

Here's another approach to getting a letter:

You hear: I really like your _____.

You say: Could you put that in writing?

You hear: Of course.

You say: Would you like me to suggest some verbiage that you might use, or would you prefer to phrase it in your own words?

There are two possibilities:

You hear: Yes, please let me know how you'd like me to say it.

You then agree to help.

or

You hear: I'd prefer to use my own words.

In either case, you're fine. However, you're not done yet. You need to establish a specific time frame for receipt of the letter.

You say: How soon do you think I might expect the letter? I don't want to inconvenience you, but the sooner I can get it, the better!

You hear: When would you like it?

You say: I'd like it by [date]. Is that acceptable?

You hear: That's fine.

    or

You hear: No, by [different date] would be better.

Either way, you're in good shape to ultimately receive a letter indicating the level of satisfaction they have with what you provided.

What should you do with the physical letter? Here are several suggestions:

- Make color copies of the original and use it in your sales presentation.
- Scan it for downloading and use it in either a digital or a hard copy format.
- Underline or highlight key words that reflect results similar to what your prospect is trying to achieve. You can do this digitally or by hand.

Requesting Testimonials via E-Mail

You might find it easier to make a request for a testimonial letter by e-mail. If that's the case, consider this approach:

You write:

George,

Just like you, we frequently have requests from prospective clients to hear from existing ones. I'm wondering if you'd consider writing a letter of recommendation about the work we did together. Because you're so busy, if it would be easier for me to put together some bullet points that you can edit, I'm happy to do that. Just let me know if you're interested and how you would like to proceed.

Looking forward to hearing back.

—Rachel

Getting Voice Mail Testimonials

For some of your clients, it is easier for them to call and leave you a voice mail testimonial. Then you transcribe their comments into writing. Send the transcript to them for their approval and ask them to place it on their letterhead.

You say: If it would be easier for you to talk about your experience, you're welcome to leave me a voice mail. Then I'll transcribe it and send it back to you for your approval. How does that sound?

You hear: That sounds good.

You say: Great. What time do you think you'll call? That way I can be sure to send you straight to voice mail.

You hear: I'll call at [time].

You say: Perfect. Thank you.

Getting Video Testimonials

You could also ask for a video or audio testimonial. These are powerful tools that can be deployed on a website, blog, or DVD.

You say: Would you be willing to allow us to videotape your thoughts about working with us and how our product has helped you?

You hear: Yes.

You say: When is the most convenient time for you to meet with us to record it?

Schedule a time that's mutually convenient.

Getting LinkedIn Recommendations

LinkedIn recommendations are valuable testimonials and can be important tools in your sales efforts. The best way to earn recommendations is by peppering your connections with sincere recommendations and then asking for the favor to be returned. Alternatively, you can ask for a recommendation from a client or colleague after providing them value.

Before sending the message via LinkedIn, ask for permission by telephone or in person. Just like asking for a referral, treat this as an important request. The more seriously you take the appeal, the more likely it is that you will receive a recommendation.

You say: Hi Sean, I'm wondering if you'd be willing to write a recommendation on LinkedIn for the work we've done for you over the past year. If so, I'll send a message through LinkedIn.

You hear: Sure. I'd be happy to. Send it on over.

You send via LinkedIn:

Sean,

Thanks so much for your willingness to write a recommendation! As you know, a lot of people visit our LinkedIn profile before agreeing to meet with us. That means recommendations are valuable tools in building the confidence potential clients will place in us and how we will be perceived.

As a result, I'm grateful for anything you're willing to say about what we accomplished together to help future clients understand what it's like to work with me.

Thanks again!

—Wes

Alternatively, you could provide more direction for the recommendation. To do that, try this approach:

You say: Would you be willing to put together a LinkedIn recommendation for me?

You hear: Definitely. What would you like me to say?

You say: I'll put together some thoughts and send it to you through LinkedIn. Then you can edit it as you see fit.

You send via LinkedIn:

Rebecca,

Thanks for agreeing to write a recommendation. Since you asked for some thoughts, here are a few things I'd be grateful to you for covering:

- What caused you to search for a provider like us?
- What caused you to select us over our competitors?
- What have you most enjoyed about working with us?
- What advice would you have for someone interested in working with us?
- Anything else you might like to cover.

Thanks!

—Phil

Conclusion

When it comes to social proof, remember the G2G philosophy. Only after providing value should you attempt to ask for social proof. But it's important to request it, because it can be one of the most powerful tools in your arsenal.

CHAPTER 10

A Long-Term Strategy

M ore than anything you do as a salesperson, adopting the Give-to-Get philosophy will have a direct impact on your sales efforts.

Handwritten Cards

Remember Sarah from Chapter 1? Her success came, in large part, from the fact that she truly lived and breathed the G2G philosophy. One of her key strategies for developing a river of referrals was sending five cards every day. She did not particularly care if it drove immediate business opportunities. Instead, she was interested in developing relationships with people who might one day provide her with connections that could lead to business opportunities. This positioning strategy led to plenty of referrals for her.

We suggest that you adopt the same goal. By sending handwritten cards you will distinguish yourself and improve your reputation, which will significantly increase your chances of earning referrals.

When a connector suggested that she contact someone, Sarah always asked these four questions:

1. What caused you to think I should meet [referral]?
2. What is [referral's] outside hobby or interest?
3. Does [referral] have something he or she is really passionate about?
4. What do you respect most about [referral]?

Armed with that information, she would send a handwritten note that followed this simple formula:

Dear [First Name],

[Connector] suggested I reach out to you. She said you [refer to something you learned from the four questions that you can relate to]. [Show your connection to that thing]. [Connector] said you were a great person to get to know. I'll

give you a call in a few days.
Sincerely,
Sarah

Without exception, she included her business card with the note.

You can do the same thing. By providing value to potential connectors, asking for referral opportunities, and following up with them, you become a more effective referral generator. In the next few pages, we share sample notes you can write. Regardless of how distant the referral is, there is always a way to highlight a connection. Take a look at these examples and commit to setting your own goals for writing these kinds of cards.

Sample Cards

If You Share Common Hobbies

Dear Jerry,
Susan suggested I reach out to you. She said that you were a great piano player. I tried taking lessons a few years ago, and now I wish I'd made more progress! Besides that, Susan said you were a great person to get to know. I'll give you a call in a few days.
Sincerely,
Thomas

If You Know of a Helpful App

Dear Clarence,
Paul suggested I reach out to you. He said you are an avid fisherman. This reminded me of an iPhone app called Rapala. Have you seen it? In any event, Paul said you were a great

person to get to know. I'll give you a call in a few days.
Sincerely,
Tim

If You Want to Volunteer with the Referral

Dear Robert,

Cooper suggested I reach out to you. He said you were passionate about your volunteer work with the Big Brothers and Big Sisters. Before I moved here, I participated in the local chapter back home. I'd love to learn about your work. Besides that, Cooper said you were a great person to get to know. I'll give you a call in a few days.

Sincerely,
Phyllis

If You Have Information to Share

Dear Steve,

Richard suggested I reach out to you. He said you were thinking about adopting a German shepherd. I've had shepherds my entire life and thought you might be interested in the article that I've enclosed. Besides that connection, Richard said you were a great person to get to know. I'll give you a call in a few days.

Sincerely,
Keith

If You Can Suggest a Book

Dear Beth,

Francine suggested I reach out to you. She said you were one of the most talented photographers she's ever met. A friend of mine recently suggested a great photography book called *The Digital Photography Book*. Have you read it? In any event,

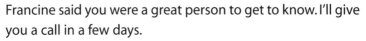

Francine said you were a great person to get to know. I'll give you a call in a few days.
Sincerely,
Lou

If You Can Suggest a Person to Meet

Dear Albert,
Christopher suggested I reach out to you. He said you were trying to meet people in the transportation business. My good friend, Luis, is the executive vice president of XYZ Transportation, Inc. I'll give you a call in a few days to find a time the three of us can get together.
Sincerely,
Mary

If You Are in the Same Club

Dear Sam,
Susan suggested I reach out to you. She said you and I are in the same Rotary Club. I can't believe we haven't met yet! Besides that connection, Susan said you were a great person to get to know. I'll give you a call in a few days.
Sincerely,
Jeff

If You Share a Common Passion

Dear Ernest,
Betty suggested I reach out to you. She said you are passionate about recycling. I share that passion. In fact, I helped start the first recycling program in my office park. Besides that, Betty said you were a great person to get to know. I'll give

you a call in a few days.
Sincerely,
Bobby

If You Have Something That Validates the Referral

Dear Lisa,

Bethany suggested I reach out to you. She said you are one of the biggest optimists she's ever met. I recently came across an article about how optimistic people live longer. I have enclosed it with this note. With that said, Bethany said that you were a great person to get to know. I'll give you a call in a few days.

Sincerely,
Miranda

If You've Taken the Same Vacation

Dear Jeff,

Wendy suggested I reach out to you. She said that you recently returned from a trip to South Africa. I traveled to Johannesburg a few years ago and would love to trade stories. Besides that, Wendy said that you were a great person to get to know. I'll give you a call in a few days.

Sincerely,
Jeffrey

If You've Worked for the Same Company

Dear Jim,

Thad suggested I reach out to you. He said that you used to work for ABC Corporation. I was there back in the 1990s and would love to swap stories. Besides that, Thad said that you were a great person to get to know. I'll give you a call in a couple of days.

Sincerely,

Lucie

If You Attended the Same School

Dear Joseph,

Haynes suggested I reach out to you. He said that you went to State College. I graduated back in 1994. I wonder whom we might know in common. Besides that, Haynes said that you were a great person to get to know. I'll give you a call in a couple of days.

Sincerely,

Christie

If You Share a Common Interest

Dear Meg,

Mike suggested I reach out to you. He said that you love gardening. I have kept a vegetable garden in my backyard for many years. Besides that, Mike said that you were a great person to get to know. I'll give you a call in a couple of days.

Sincerely,

Alison

If Your Children Go to the Same School

Dear Peter,

Mary Beth suggested I reach out to you. She said that your children are at Northern Elementary. My daughter Ashley is in Ms. Schwartz's third grade class. Besides that, Mary Beth said that you were a great person to get to know. I'll give you

a call in a few days.
Sincerely,
Terry

If You Have Lived in the Same Place

Dear Harry,

Kevin suggested I reach out to you. He said that you used to live in Syracuse. I lived there for a few years back in the late 1990s. Besides that, Kevin said that you were a great person to get to know. I'll give you a call in a couple of days.

Sincerely,

Tony

If You Have Served on a Board of Directors

Dear Rich,

Preston suggested I reach out to you. He said that you are serving on the United Way Board of Directors. I served there a few years ago and would love to share some ideas and learn about what is happening now. Besides that, Preston said that you were a great person to get to know. I'll give you a call in a few days.

Sincerely,

Alan

CHAPTER 11

Conclusion

We have worked hard to pack the latest research related to contemporary selling into this book. However, never lose sight of the reality that it is not what you say that matters; what really matters is how you say it.

Earning referrals is all about deploying the right strategy, saying the right things, and then saying those things in the right way. Frankly communicating the right way means using tone, speed, and sincerity. So remember: it's not only what you say, but how you say it. That's a crucial distinction.

You should also consider what not to say. You've invested a great deal of effort into learning the strategies and phrases in this book. Don't fall victim to old school statements that people hope will generate referrals. These include things like

Don't Say: Can you think of someone who needs a new car?

Don't Say: The next time you know someone who needs the help I provide, think of me.

Don't Say: Can you think of someone who needs financial planning?

Don't Say: When you think of successful people who would like to meet me, who comes to mind?

Don't Say: Can you think of someone who needs new accounting software?

Don't Say: Why don't you introduce me to your three best friends.

Don't Say: Let's take a look at your LinkedIn connections and see whom you can introduce me to.

Don't Say: Can you think of someone who needs a new home?

Why do these phrases fail? Because they don't account for the Give-to-Get philosophy. Instead, they are uncomfortable for your connector and create resistance rather than build a willingness to provide quality referrals.

Now, here's a challenge for you. Are you prepared to earn referrals in a positive, productive way every single day? Are you ready to Give-to-Get? And this challenge applies to you however sophisticated you may be, however complex your sales cycle, whatever the price point of your product or service, and whatever level of service your offering demands of you.

Why is that? Remember: The secret to selling is to be in front of a prospective customer when he or she is ready to buy, not when you need to make a sale.

It has been a pleasure for us to write this book. We hope that you find its content to be as valuable to you as it has been to us. These are the same strategies, tactics, and phrases that we use daily in our sales careers. Our sales team uses these tools—and we have trained hundreds of thousands of salespeople to use them worldwide as well. Now they're yours. Use them wisely!

The Right Phrase for
Every Situation...Every Time

Perfect Phrases for Building Strong Teams
Perfect Phrases for Business Letters
Perfect Phrases for Business Proposals and Business Plans
Perfect Phrases for Business School Acceptance
Perfect Phrases for College Application Essays
Perfect Phrases for Cover Letters
Perfect Phrases for Customer Service
Perfect Phrases for Dealing with Difficult People
Perfect Phrases for Dealing with Difficult Situations at Work
Perfect Phrases for Documenting Employee Performance Problems
Perfect Phrases for Executive Presentations
Perfect Phrases for Landlords and Property Managers
Perfect Phrases for Law School Acceptance
Perfect Phrases for Lead Generation
Perfect Phrases for Managers and Supervisors
Perfect Phrases for Managing Your Small Business
Perfect Phrases for Medical School Acceptance
Perfect Phrases for Meetings
Perfect Phrases for Motivating and Rewarding Employees
Perfect Phrases for Negotiating Salary & Job Offers
Perfect Phrases for Perfect Hiring
Perfect Phrases for the Perfect Interview
Perfect Phrases for Performance Reviews
Perfect Phrases for Real Estate Agents & Brokers
Perfect Phrases for Resumes
Perfect Phrases for Sales and Marketing Copy
Perfect Phrases for the Sales Call
Perfect Phrases for Sales Presentations
Perfect Phrases for Setting Performance Goals
Perfect Phrases for Small Business Owners
Perfect Phrases for the TOEFL Speaking and Writing Sections
Perfect Phrases for Writing Company Announcements
Perfect Phrases for Writing Grant Proposals
Perfect Phrases in American Sign Language for Beginners
Perfect Phrases in French for Confident Travel
Perfect Phrases in German for Confident Travel
Perfect Phrases in Italian for Confident Travel
Perfect Phrases in Spanish for Confident Travel to Mexico
Perfect Phrases in Spanish for Construction
Perfect Phrases in Spanish for Gardening and Landscaping

Visit mhprofessional.com/perfectphrases for a complete product listing.

Learn more. Do more.

About the Authors

Jeb Brooks is president of The Brooks Group, an award-winning sales training firm that helps organizations improve their sales effectiveness by providing sales and sales management assessment, training, and retention services. In addition, he manages and writes for The Brooks Group's Sales Evolution Blog. Connect with him at LinkedIn.com/in/JebBrooks.

Marty Scirratt is an author, speaker and executive consultant. The former senior vice president of sales at a publicly traded firm, he led a team of 500 people responsible for more than $1.7 billion in sales, much of it referral-based. Marty and his wife Leslie live in North Carolina, spending much of their time supporting and working with their favorite charities and causes. Connect with him at www.LinkedIn.com/in/MartyScirratt.